# ALL IT TAKES IS A LITTLE
# more... GUMPTION

# ALL IT TAKES IS A LITTLE more... GUMPTION

## Lisa Blake

NEW HOLLAND

# Dedicated to...

My two little dreamers, Luca and Nate.
All for one and one for all, Boo and Moo.

*Sweet dreams*
till sunbeams find you
*Sweet dreams*
that leave all worries behind you
But in your
*dreams*
whatever they be
*Dream a little dream*
*of me.*

'Dream a Little Dream of Me', lyrics by Gus Kahn, 1931

# CONTENTS

# Foreword

# Lisa Blake is one of the most inspiring women I know.

Right from the moment I met Lisa, I have been moved by her drive, her incredible achievements and, above all, her huge heart. To have been left in a heart-wrenching position and to decide to dream a little dream instead of giving up is just a small part of what makes her so extraordinary. You will get to know Lisa and her story in the pages of this uplifting book – and I know you will love her immensely, just the way I did the day we met.

Lisa has impacted thousands of people with her story: she demonstrates that it is possible to turn your life into one you love, no matter how you are feeling or where you are right now. She shows us what strength looks like and lives as an example of how challenge can define, not defeat us. And she aspires every day to help women (and men) to dream their little dream and make it happen.

Just by being who she is, Lisa inspires me to be who I truly am, share my gifts with the world and keep dreaming regardless of the bumps in the road. She speaks up for causes that matter, puts her love and heart into her business and family, and is the kind of woman of whom the world needs more.

It has been an inspiration to support Lisa on the journey of writing what I believe is the first of many books. I am truly blessed to call her a friend and fellow sister on a mission to make a difference in the lives of those who need it most.

With inspiration,

*Emily Gowor*
*Inspirational author and speaker*

# INTRODUCTION

Growing up, it is in our genetic make-up as conscious beings to fantasise about how life will be: with whom we will spend it, the career we will pursue and the family we will create and nurture.

**W**hile some of those visions come true, more often than not, life doesn't turn out the way we plan. I don't know about you, but I can say I'm not surrounded by a lot of people who proclaim: 'Yes! That's pretty much *exactly* how I thought life would turn out for me.'

Now, life throwing us surprises is half the fun and not having everything mapped out makes being here on Earth a wonderful adventure. But I have always been a dreamer about what will be and, up until my early 30s, I was pretty certain that I was fulfilling the vision I'd cast for myself as a young girl.

It won't come as a surprise to you that not once did I dream I'd be an unemployed single mum of two little boys in my late 30s. That's not a dream, is it? That's a complete nightmare!

Back then, I was pretty sure this sort of reality doesn't happen to school prefects who are educated, work hard and who grew up in a stable household.

Or does it?

Yes. It turns out it does.

Because it happened to me.

The last four years of my life have been a hotpot of overwhelming devastation and amazing excitement all at once. One day I was kicking career goals with an international PR career and was a proud mum of a beautiful little boy, with a supportive partner to help me out. The next, I was an unemployed single mum of two little boys under three, one of whom was fighting for his life as a preemie in the Neonatal Intensive Care Unit (NICU).

Now, I'm all up for change, but this was just too much. It was like the universe was playing a sick joke on me. I kept hoping I'd wake up and see it was just a dream. A big, fat, ugly one, but nonetheless, a dream.

But it was real life - it was MY real life - and the eternal optimist in me suddenly felt defeated. Have you ever had that feeling? It's almost worse than what's happening, knowing that your positive spirit has been beaten to the point where you can't see anything good left.

Fast forward to today, and I am an entrepreneur with an award-winning business. I've built a new house for my family less than three years after I walked into Centrelink (an Australian government agency) for single parent benefits. And I met one of my entrepreneurial idols in person less than a year after I made that goal publicly known on my bucket list.

How did I do it? I won the lottery!

Ah, if only it was that easy. I don't even buy lottery tickets, so there's a flaw in that plan right there. And let's be honest, this book would be pretty dull and short if that'd happened.

What I *really* did may make you furrow your brow and cock your head to one side… but it's the truth.

**All I did was dream small.**

**Yes, that's right. I decided to dream *little* dreams.**

If, back when my life was a mess, I'd dreamt about a massive house in St Tropez, a Porsche in the driveway and millions in the bank so I could do whatever I wanted every day, I can tell you now it would have only added to my misery.

Instead, these little dreams were ones I could touch and see so clearly. I knew I could actually achieve them if I just stayed focused and took action and had the gumption[1] to see it through.

This may sound dramatic, but in moments of darkness and despair, little dreams saved my little boys and me from sliding further down the black hole of inaction and, even worse still, inertia.

---

1   You'll note I have used the word 'gumption' on the front cover of this book. Defined as 'shrewd or spirited initiative and resourcefulness' it's a critical ingredient in little dreams coming true.

## Dreaming Little Was the
## Panacea to my Predicament

It's really important as you step through the pages of this book to remember that everyone starts dreaming small. As the saying goes:

### 'Don't judge your page 1 against
### someone else's page 500.'

Beyoncé did not wake up on day one of her life a world-famous pop star with an existence that looks pretty freaking awesome, from the outside in. Barack Obama wasn't born in the White House as President of the United States, ready to reign as the leader of the free world. Richard Branson didn't inherit several successful businesses, all ready to go, and get gifted Necker Island.

While I've only met one of these people in person (and I'll tell you ALL about that in the coming pages), I am going to hazard a guess that they started with some little dreams first; ones that kept their motivation and self-belief levels high and, once achieved, helped contribute to the creation of a life they love living every day.

We also live in times where our external world can deliver events we don't expect on a global scale (COVID-19, anyone), and little dreams are perhaps even more important. Unsurprisingly, I applied the same little dreams philosophy to this larger reality check and the results have been interesting. I'll share more in the last two chapters.

# MY WISH FOR YOU

With this book, I also want YOU to retrain your mind to dream little.

Go on, take the pressure off.

I believe dreams should be attainable in the scope of your capabilities and reflect where you are right now. It doesn't matter what your current personal situation is; little dreams are relevant to us all because they are a powerful way to get out of the drudgery and into a beautiful space where your heart sings, your face smiles and you simply love being alive.

I honestly don't want to know about your big dreams. There are plenty of books and websites that can help you with that. I'm not saying you can't or shouldn't dream big – I still do this, as little dreams all contribute to the bigger ones, plus it's heaps of fun!

But from my own life experience I know that a big dream doesn't change right here, right now. They have the very real potential to overwhelm even the most optimistic among us and generate a feeling of apathy because 'as if that's ever going to be ME' or 'as if I'll ever achieve that.'

I invite you to take my hand while I accompany you on my journey over the last four years, sharing  how I overcame the challenges life threw me with this seemingly upside down strategy.

**The social proof – the validation I'm onto something with my counterintuitive 'dream little' philosophy – is my own life and the dramatic, positive change in my reality over just four years.**

You're in safe hands with me because I have lived and road-tested every single recommendation inside these pages. I can show you, through my raw honesty about what happened and what I did, that my approach actually works.

Don't get too comfortable though: even little dreams require significant effort, commitment and elbow grease. They don't have legs and arms. They're not going to walk up to your house, knock on the door and yell: *'Surprise! I'm here!'* (I know; it's cute to think of dreams that way, isn't it?).

It is my fervent hope that my life experience, combined with a firm sprinkle of your own magic and big dollops of action, will bring the same wonderful outcomes for you that dreaming small delivered for me. The techniques I share openly are those that anyone, regardless of life circumstances, can implement starting today. Yes - TODAY. I believe showing you my world then and now will be all you need to see that you can do it too.

**Essentially, this book is a guiding hand through the fog; a template roadmap for you to personalise so you too can realise your little dreams.**

## LET'S START NOW. YES, TODAY!

So, I'm assuming we are on the same page (metaphorically, because literally we most certainly are!). We agree that life is a series of moments and we only have right now. So why wouldn't you choose to make this one right now as happy as possible, by dreaming little and changing the dial on your barometer of satisfaction closer to the top of the scale?

The wise old soul Confucius is quoted as saying: *'It doesn't matter how slowly you go, as long as you do not stop.'* So, let's start slowly, right now.

Because dreams are very different for all of us, it's super important I give you some guidance on what a little dream is, versus a big one.

## THE DNA OF A LITTLE DREAM

- It forms one part of a much bigger dream. For example, if you want to start a business, a little dream may be to confirm what you're offering is viable amongst the target audience; if you want to have a holiday home overseas, a little dream may be to reach a financial target for the deposit.
- It can be realistically achieved within a year.
  Any longer than that, forget it - it's not a little dream, it's a vague wish.
- You have all you need at your disposal to make it

happen – connections, resources, skills, knowledge and critically, gumption!

- You whole-heartedly believe it can come true; that you can bring it to fruition.
- Most importantly of all, when you think about it you get butterflies in your tummy, like you did when Santa was coming the next morning. This is because you can feel it, see it and *almost* touch it.

## WHAT LITTLE DREAMS DO YOU WANT TO COME TRUE IN THE NEXT YEAR?

So, now we've defined the DNA of a Little Dream, it's time for you to put a stake in the virtual ground. Capture your thoughts now because, once you dive into this book, you'll want to start taking action to achieve them straight away!

Go and grab a notebook and pen or write in the space provided below.

### *MY LITTLE DREAM WISH LIST*

1._____

2. _____

3. _____

4. _____

5._____

6. _____

*(Remember, you'll know it's a little dream if you feel like you did on Christmas morning or a similar exciting occasion when you were*

*younger. That child-like excitement is always a good sign you're onto something amazing.)*

As you read this book, check back on what you've captured now and refine as you need to.

Also keep in the back of your mind the fact that I am just an ordinary person who believes I deserve the extraordinary and decided to go for it, one little dream at a time. This very book, which you now have nestled in your hands, is a testament to that! It's taken two years to get through nine versions of the manuscript (as Ernest Hemingway famously said: 'The first draft of anything is shit' – and he's right!), and at least as many versions of the cover and inside artwork to get to this finished product. But I kept dreaming small, ticking each milestone off as I reached it and here I am.

Here YOU are!

And you deserve the extraordinary too.

So, are you in?

Are you ready?

Good.

# Let's go and make some little dreams come true.

# The End Before the Beginning

Imagine you're reading a script for a new show on TV. All the characters are listed with their key personality trait so you immediately understand where they fit into the broader narrative. Next to the character of Lisa Burling you'd see these words: 'The quintessential good girl'.

My parents never had to worry about me because I did everything by the book and stayed out of trouble. I was always the teacher's pet, finished school with excellent grades, went to university to study journalism and public relations, got a great job straight away (and continued to get great jobs) and, excitingly, moved from Australia to London at twenty-three years of age to further my career.

I had a fantastic circle of friends in countries all over the world, a high disposable income and a loving family: I had it all.

That version of me was one hell of a go-getter. My PR career in London spanned a decade and I was working on some of the world's biggest global brands, as well as leading PR for the charitable arm of the Royal College of Obstetricians & Gynaecologists. I'd travelled to many parts of the world, meeting celebrities like Mick Jagger and hanging out with the team who delivered Prince William, as if it was just another day at the office. Because it was!

Every day was such an adventure and I was surrounded by highly ambitious people who pushed me forward to be the best version of myself. Life was good. Really good.

When I reached thirty-three, after ten years living away from home, I felt the pull to go back. London was never the long-term option and, on the inside, I felt like my time there had expired. I also heard my biological clock ticking louder each year. I missed my family and I was tired of missing out on the big stuff – weddings, birthdays, births – and the little stuff, like coffee catch-ups on Sunday morning.

So I packed up my life in Old Blighty and came back to the land Down Under. It felt right and I was pleased to be on Aussie soil again. I started working at a leading Sydney PR consultancy and loved being in close proximity to people I'd only see once a year when I came back/home to visit from London. Life was still good. Really good.

Then, in a seemingly random chain of events, I reconnected with an old flame from high school. And that's when my life began to morph into something very different.

With this man, who I'd known since childhood, I embarked on a love affair that I honestly thought would last a lifetime. In just three years, we had a baby (my beautiful Luca, in March 2011) and I moved my professional career from Sydney to Kiama, a beautiful but small town about two hours south of Sydney.

In quiet moments, I wasn't entirely sure how I'd got to this place where the pace was much slower than I was used to, both literally and metaphorically. Sure, I'd made the decisions, but it didn't feel like they were truly conscious ones. I wasn't in the driver's seat; I was simply agreeing with what the car's driver was suggesting.

Regardless of these thoughts, I talked myself into believing that this was what I should be doing in my mid-thirties. I was a mum now and that meant I couldn't have a high-flying PR career anymore. My role was to be the homemaker and support my partner as he earned the big bucks.

I wasn't unhappy, and I was so grateful to be a mum, but I was unfulfilled. Something just didn't feel right about the situation. And yet, I kept convincing myself that I was where I was meant to be. I was thirty-five and I'd had my fun. What goes up must come down. I was also never going to unravel this reality: I didn't want to break my little family up just because I felt a bit bored. That didn't seem like a good enough reason to turn my life in a completely new or different direction.

Yet, it seems that the universe heard me, saw me, *felt* me. Something wasn't right and what happened next, all of it completely outside of my control, changed my life path forever.

> 'When you veer off your life path,
> the universe will see you, hear you and feel you,
> to get you back on track.'

It was October 2013 and I was in the second trimester of my second pregnancy. As many women will attest, the second time around is often completely different. I suffered a miscarriage between my two babies and when I did fall pregnant the second time, it was stressful from the start. My first baby, Luca was textbook; I was happy and healthy and felt extremely privileged to be 'over the hill' in the professional eyes of my obstetrician, yet able to grow and bring into the world a perfect little bub, my Luca, at the ripe old age of thirty-five.

Not long after falling pregnant for the third time, I was diagnosed with placenta previa, a condition that means the placenta has implanted at the bottom of the uterus, over the cervix or close by. Put simply, this means the baby can't get out the usual way. It can be a small inconvenience, or it can be a big problem. For me, it was the latter. I had the last stage, stage four. This meant I felt unwell all the time, with a constant fear that my baby could fall out at any time, which was truly odd as there was no way he could get out through the normal exit. I also had extreme nausea, and so I felt like I was in a tiny boat in a massive swell 24/7.

Simultaneously, my relationship wasn't in a healthy place. The excitement that comes with a new love had well and truly faded by then and we were both knee-deep in the day-to-day drudgery so commonly associated with working and having a small baby. Without a solid foundation of love and mutual respect, it was going to be hard to keep it together.

We were disconnected on many levels but didn't ever talk about it. I didn't raise the topic because I was scared of what talking about it would bring up. It is one thing to work through silly little misunderstandings, but quite another to work through a complete misalignment of values and life direction. I know we both felt misunderstood and frustrated as we came to a collective, silent realisation that, for us, high school romances were probably best left at the school gate.

Yet, ever the optimist, I had convinced myself that once this second baby made it Earth-side, we'd address our relationship and get things back on track. I'd have two children, my partner, and life would be perfect: just as it should be. Exactly as I'd dreamed it would be. Broken relationships when children were involved just didn't happen to people like me.

'Mum, I'm bleeding. I need to get to the hospital.'

I was thirty-two weeks pregnant when I yelled those words. My partner was away on a soccer cruise and I was petrified. I'd read about the chances of premature birth being higher with placenta previa, but who thinks they'll actually be one of the statistics? I certainly didn't … until that moment.

I knew that this baby was coming. I also knew that the only way I was going to get through it was to eat the elephant one bite at a time. My mum shared this concept with me years earlier as a way to break down a seemingly insurmountable or complex task into chunks that are manageable and achievable.

---

'Eating the elephant one bite at a time is sometimes the only way to make a seemingly insurmountable or complex task achievable.'

---

At that point, eating the elephant was simply getting to the hospital and seeing my obstetrician. Nothing else mattered but the wellbeing of the little baby inside of me.

As soon as I got to the hospital, they whisked me in for a scan. Good news. He was OK (I knew it was a boy at this point). His little heart was beating and he was moving. The bad news was his respiratory system was not yet fully formed and that meant every single minute he spent inside the warm cocoon of my body counted.

My obstetrician arrived not long after and she explained the most common lung problem in a premature baby is respiratory distress syndrome (RDS), which occurs when the lungs don't produce sufficient amounts of surfactant (a substance that keeps the tiny air sacs in the lung open). Our aim was to keep him inside as long as possible so his little lungs could develop. He was given an injection of surfactant as extra help. I was envisaging spending eight weeks in a hospital bed, lying still and horizontal. That I could cope with. Thoughts of a premature baby and having to spend weeks worrying about his survival in hospital were too much to contemplate at that point.

Less than twenty-four hours later, I went into full-blown labour. The contractions were thick and fast and there was no question that this baby was about to arrive. You know the saying 'A little knowledge is a dangerous thing'? I'd read far too much about premature birth and placenta previa and I was convinced I'd die when they conducted the emergency caesarean because extreme blood loss is a huge possibility.

As always, I slapped on a brave face, hugged my tummy and, although not an overly religious person, I prayed.

The truth is I remember very little about what happened next. I remember thinking completely trivial stuff like 'I should have had a bikini wax' and 'My feet need a pedicure'. Far more importantly, I vividly remember my obstetrician holding my little boy above the green screen and saying, 'Lisa, he's here. Your little boy is here.' He screamed that newborn scream that you wait for as you hold your own breath, and I relaxed just a little.

*He's here*, I thought. *Thank you*, I mouthed silently as the amazing team of doctors and nurses got to work putting me back together and hooking him up to an intricate maze of cords and devices.

'I think we should call him Nate,' his dad said before he left the operating theatre. I was out of it but agreed with a nod. Even in my drug-induced, shocked state, I knew this little boy was destined to have this name. He was our little neonate; it was the perfect name.

That was the last time his dad and I decided on anything together for a long time.

## Beep. Beep. Beep.

The sound of the machines monitoring my little baby's heart and vital signs in the Neonatal Intensive Care Unit (NICU) were relentless, monotonous and, to be honest, cold. Watching Nate fight with every breath and grappling with my own abdominal pain as I dealt with the aftermath of an emergency caesarean was like hell on Earth for me. I was in a complete state of shock at the depths of despair in which I had found myself. I didn't know which pain to deal with, so I decided I wouldn't deal with any of it and allow the numbness to override me. I was existing out of my own body, every second of every day.

Unbeknownst to me, I'd mastered the observer state we read about in books by spiritual leaders who claim it is the ultimate way of being and the path to happiness. I can categorically tell you I wasn't feeling anywhere near the path to happiness at this time; I was simply stepping outside of myself because being inside my own existence was too painful and way too damn sad.

Nate was tucked in his humidicrib with tubes everywhere, his little chest going up and down, up and down, like a buoy on the sea that can't decide if it's high tide or low tide.

I took photos and shared them on social media. The way I framed them didn't convey how tiny he was and that was entirely on purpose.

I whacked filters on the images to hide the fact he was jaundiced. I didn't want to have to deal with comments about his teeny structure or strange colouring; I wanted him to be a normal-sized baby, a healthy one. The baby clothes I'd bought for him were at home, on top of a cot still inside its box. There had been no time to pack a bag; he wouldn't be big enough to wear 0000 for at least two months anyway.

When you are a parent to a preemie, worry is your constant companion. Just because there are more occurrences of premature birth today – or maybe we just talk about it more so it seems that way – it doesn't make the actual experience any less scary. I simply couldn't relax and I took no comfort in the nurses reassuring me Nate was doing OK.

My anxiety was through the roof and life became very small. When you're in the NICU, the lights are dim and, despite their robotic precision, the beeps of the C-PAP machine became strangely meditative. You step into a bubble focused solely on keeping tiny babies alive.

I wore PJs all day in the hospital. I didn't care about getting my 'pre-baby body' back like I did with Luca; I didn't care about my body at all. I recognise this is really superficial stuff but when you start to let basic personal care go, it's a pretty good indicator of how you're actually feeling inside.

## Little did I know, things were about to get a whole lot worse.

Nate had been alive for just forty-eight hours. I reluctantly left his side to have a quick shower in my room. This particular day, I was recovering from my own operation and feeling very unwell; unlike the previous two days, I couldn't busy myself out of the pain I was feeling. A shower always made me feel a little better, even though it was a fleeting feeling.

An hour before I'd noticed a phone call from Nate's dad; I'd assumed he was calling to see how I was and perhaps come to the hospital. I called him back, thinking it was a check-in call.

I'll never, ever forget that moment when I called him back, in that shower room, in that hospital, on that day.

After a few questions about how Nate was, he dropped a bomb on me: he was out – he was leaving me. It wasn't working, he wasn't happy and that was it.

Done and dusted.

I felt like I was in one of those American TV shows, where everyone stands still and then goes, 'Ha! We got you!' before rolling around laughing hysterically and backslapping each other on a job well done. Maybe Ashton Kutcher was about to jump out and tell me I'd been punk'd. But it wasn't a movie and Ashton was nowhere to be seen.

I hung up, took a deep breath and I sobbed on the floor of a cold, impersonal hospital room for what was probably five minutes, but seemed to be hours.

Of course, I didn't fully accept this fate straight away. In fact, I was so drugged up on pain-relief medication, I almost dismissed the fact that the call had even taken place. It helped that I was understandably very diverted by the important task of keeping my child alive and myself well enough to breastfeed him. Quite frankly, I didn't have the time, nor the energy, to worry too much about his dad and that call at all in the days and weeks that followed. My days and weeks became a comforting stream of tasks that focused me away from dealing with anything emotional. I was a fembot.

After the first week of being in my hospital room down the hall from Nate, the hospital staff told me I had to go home. Leaving Nate in the hospital was incredibly hard; it's just not how things should be. I offered to pay to stay there, clearly forgetting it was a hospital, not a hotel. I packed my bags reluctantly and made the nurses in the

NICU promise they'd watch Nate like he was one of their own, now that I wasn't a hop, skip and a jump down the hallway. Of course they promised; I'm convinced all nurses have angel wings we can't see.

At this time, to make it logistically easier, Luca and I relocated to Mum and Dad's house as it was closer to the hospital. I also won't deny that I rather naively assumed space from the boys' dad might make him miss me (it didn't). I'd get up each morning, give Luca huge kisses and hugs, and my dad would drive me to the NICU (I was still unable to drive because of my emergency caesarean). Once I was inside the NICU, I'd feed and bath Nate, cuddle him for as long as I was allowed to (I had to ask permission from the nurses to hold my own baby), leave when he was asleep for an hour, go back and watch him, feed him again, talk to the nurses or another parent so I felt like a normal human being, and stay next to him until the nurses told me I had to go.

Most days, when I'd get home to my parents' house from the NICU, I'd have tears streaming down my face out of sadness, frustration and sheer exhaustion. My parents didn't know these tears were also because of the situation with the boys' dad. I just couldn't face burdening them with that and I really thought I could make it better, once Nate was home.

Each night I'd lie in the bedroom I'd grown up in as a child, the same room in which I'd dreamt about my future, and wonder how I was in this awful situation. I thought constantly about Nate, up in that hospital next to other preemies, and cried into my pillow because I couldn't see him or touch him. I had my phone glued to my hand and slept in small bursts.

The nurses would often call me during the night or early morning and, every time, I was convinced something bad had happened and that Nate had been taken from me. In most cases it was a call to let me know he was awake and crying and wanted to be fed. But you never, ever get complacent or expect the best in these situations.

The day finally came when the nurses at the NICU let me know his paediatrician would be coming by to see if Nate was ready to be discharged. They were happy with his weight and felt he was well enough to be with me, and his brother, outside of a 24/7 medical care environment. I was euphoric when Nate's discharge was confirmed.

An enormous weight shifted. I was proud of us. We were going home.

℘℘

As the energy spent worrying about Nate constantly became available for use elsewhere, I directed it to the other rather large concern I had: the tatters that were now my life. How the hell was I going to rebuild it? Where on Earth did I even begin? Could I make the boys' dad love me again? Was our little family really torn apart, never to be put back together again? How was I going to earn money? Where would we live? The questions were relentless, yet the answers were nowhere to be found.

I knew nothing except this: I had to get real with myself and face the cold-hard facts. My old life wasn't coming back, ever. I was, in this moment, nothing more than Lisa Burling, an unemployed, single mum of two little boys under the age of three.

**Lisa Burling. Single mum. Unemployed.**

Once I connected the dots and pieced together this new fractured identity, I suddenly felt so tired. I was tired of pretending I was OK; that my life was OK. I didn't give in or give up on me, but it's fair to say my mental, emotional and physical exhaustion forced my hand. And, amongst the exhaustion, I started to feel what is best described as a shift, an acceptance. I had no fight left in me and was definitely over wishing for life to be as it had been.

In the fog that was my mind, I somehow understood how important it was to separate what I could control from what I couldn't. I reminded myself how short our time on this Earth is and that this was not how I wanted to remember my life on my deathbed. I slowly but surely put aside the sheer disbelief of it all, as hard as that was.

I asked myself: 'Why not me? Why not now?' I also asked the universe if I could use this situation to make good. I just *knew* this was not how my life was meant to be. I could somehow see this darkness was cracking me open in the short term, to allow the light to shine from within me in the long-term.

I reconciled that my little boy had made an early entrance, one that would shake up my entire world and rip the foundations from underneath me, because he was meant to. It's like he'd been sent from the heavens by my spirit guides and angels to get me back to my destiny, with his fighting spirit firmly tucked under reed-thin arms in an imaginary backpack no one could see yet. Even in his humidicrib, those black eyes would sometimes stare out at me to say, 'I *know* all of this, Mum. I get this Earth stuff, I really do, and I'll be more than fine. You will too.'

I firmly decided that, instead of seeing this perceived utter catastrophe as a bad thing and an end, I should change the lens and view it as chance to start again. Like a blank Etch A Sketch, I'd been given an almighty shake, and now it was blank, well, pretty much anything was possible.

New beginnings don't come along all the time, and here I was with one sitting right in my lap if I was brave enough to go for it; to let go of what was and what might have been, and step firmly into what could be.

> 'New beginnings don't come along all the time; let go of what was and what might have been, and step firmly into what could be.'

I did what I felt was the *only* thing that made any sense to me in that moment.

**I started to dream little.**

Big dreams are easy to articulate,
but hard to achieve.
Conversely, little dreams
are harder to identify,
but easier to make come true.

*All they need to come to life?*

*A clear plan and consistent action.*

# PART 1

## Dreaming of ...
## BEING BRAVE

*You can step into the unknown to survive ... and thrive*

# 01

# BETWEEN

# MY FLOCK AND MY TREASURE

So, now I was on my own. There was no chance of my relationship being fixed. He'd left and it was just me. I was suddenly promoted to every top job going - chief decision maker, chief financial officer ... chief of everything officer. Two little boys needed me, and they needed me to reconfigure a life so different to what I'd dreamt of ... really fast.

During the darkest moments following Nate's arrival, I was always acutely aware I was unemployed. This was a first for me. My pa always said to me, 'Never leave a job without one to go to, Treasure.' I could have argued that I had an unpaid job as mum to Luca and Nate, so technically I'd stuck to his advice. But, this technicality aside, having an income to support us was high on the list of things to deal with once I'd accepted my single mum status.

I'd come from a six-figure salary reality working in senior roles in global PR consultancies. Now? My parents were giving me money to buy food. It was a situation that was nothing short of embarrassing and heartbreaking. I was constantly thinking: 'How did I get here? *How*?'

At this time, I had to swallow my pride even further, as much as it hurt to do so, and contact Centrelink (the Australian Government social security payments program) to go on single parent benefits. This was the moment I learnt what the saying 'short-term pain for long-term gain' *really* meant.

I'd been to this place before to get Paid Parental Leave and that was a pleasant visit. This was not: for the first time, I had to verbalise out loud my single parent status to a complete stranger. My ticket number was called and off I went to a desk nestled tightly between many others. As I opened my mouth, I started to sob. Sitting opposite me was a man with a soft Cockney accent. Seeing the fierce relentlessness of the salty tears falling from my eyes and the snot dripping from my nose, he handed me tissues across the desk. I must have looked like something inside of me was dying, because what saved me from completely collapsing was the reaction he had to my reality.

'It's OK love,' he said. 'Just remember, this isn't forever. See it as a helping hand for now that you can let go of, when you're ready. That's all this is for you; a pit stop on the journey.'

How lucky was I to have that man, with that attitude, greet me at that moment? I just knew I was being looked out for by forces greater than myself at Centrelink that day. It also didn't escape me this man had an accent that reminded me of my days in London, when I was myself and powering on in life.

Once I'd completed the enormous amount of paperwork required to get a tiny payment each fortnight, I said goodbye to the man who had been so kind to me and stepped out into what was a glorious day. I decided to take just ten minutes to process what had happened, and wandered across the road to a park.

I sat down on a bench, and pulled out my phone, for which my parents were also paying. I've always loved setting future diary dates for myself, as I like to see if what I predict comes true. On that particular day, as the sun was on my back and I sat for those short ten minutes, I wrote myself a diary date for six months' time. The future date was 29 July 2014. What did it say?

'See? I told you things would get better!'

When I was in my incredibly angry and frustrated phase, which hit between Nate coming out of the NICU and me deciding what to do now my life was a completely blank canvas, I beat myself up because I thought I'd wasted all those years building an international PR career and impressive CV. That was the lens through which I was looking at my life, and I was sticking to that story at that time. Being angry with myself somehow made me feel better and I was exceptionally good at it. Feeling sorry for myself was comforting too, as unlike everything else about my life, I could control it.

> Being angry at yourself can make you feel better; there is a comfort in it, especially when everything else about your life is completely out of control.

For a few weeks, I well and truly gave up on ever reacquainting myself with the career woman who'd been slowly watered down to non-existence. I started to see a future in my mind's eye where I'd get a part-time job requiring basic administration skills: no pressure, no enjoyment. Just a pay cheque each week to cover the basics of staying alive for my boys and me. I even contemplated delivering catalogues in my neighbourhood because that's all I felt I was worth, and all I thought I could practically do with two little humans needing me 24/7.

Yet there was still a fire in me, still some embers keeping a light on. I started, almost involuntarily, to picture a virtual suitcase filled with useful things that could help me through this difficult time, and in there, front and centre, was my PR career: my qualifications, knowledge, experience and contacts. It was dawning on me, slowly but surely, that perhaps I could earn money doing what I was good at, and I could possibly do it in a framework that allowed me to be a present, active mum to Luca and Nate at the same time. Perhaps I could be my own boss.

Every day, I'd contemplate this kernel of an idea and it started to take shape, just like a baby inside the womb. As I fed Nate, as I dressed Luca, as I walked them to the park, as I had my shower, as I mentally counted the cost of the food going in my trolley to ensure I had enough cash to actually pay for it. It was a relentless thought that I just couldn't push to the back of my head, no matter how hard I tried.

I'm often asked how I came to think about setting up something on my own as an option. My answer is always the same – I *felt* it. It seems an inadequate response to give to someone who's looking for meaty details but that's the honest truth. I felt it like an electric current running through my heart, my bones and my veins. Of course I had worked in the PR industry for many years, established a network of connections and developed my expertise, so I knew that I had the foundations of a successful business. But I didn't seek out this crazy idea or invite it in; the thought just appeared and, like a squatter, I couldn't get rid of it easily, if at all.

> You know you're following your life path when it feels like an electric current running through your veins. You don't seek it or invite the thought in; it just appears and, like a squatter, you can't get rid of it easily, if at all.

Call it divine intervention, call it sleep-deprived insanity, it doesn't matter. Upon reflection, it hit me hardest when I sat in my breastfeeding rocking chair with Nate at 2 am and looked at his tiny frame and perfect face. That's really where the idea took shape. So, in retrospect, yes: it probably was more sleep-deprived insanity than a message from the heavens.

Regardless of how the thought came to be, I knew I had to at the very least *explore* the idea of a professional reality where I worked for me, keeping us financially afloat and allowing me to go to things like the preschool Parents' Day, even if it was just for six months until I found a proper job. There's no harm or pressure just exploring and pondering, right? The worst that could happen had already happened, so what did I have to lose?

The 'pros and cons list' is my go-to strategy when I need help to guide my thinking. I was doing this well before it became the calling card of new-age spiritual gurus because it makes a heap of sense. I grabbed a pen and paper, knowing my heart speaks to me when I actually write things down.

In this scenario, there were two possible choices:

- **Option A:** an in-house PR job working for someone else, or
- **Option B:** being my own boss for a while, running a business in a way that would allow me to be both a mum to my very little children and make enough money for us to survive. (I used the word survive on purpose because it really was a hand-to-mouth situation back then.)

Option A had so many pros and the cons where fairly limited, although lack of flexibility to be there for my boys was a big negative. It was without a doubt the sensible choice and I actually went so far as to apply for in-house PR manager roles just before Nate was discharged. I got an interview for each, but after setting up times and preparing, I rang each prospective employer and pulled out. I was so thankful to them for the interview, but I just couldn't do it; it felt so against my life direction.

Option B? Running my own business? Wowsers. The cons were off the scale. There were so many I pretty much stopped writing them down. I'd never run a business, so what the hell did I know about what was required? That fear-based-thinking monster reared its big, ugly head. If I'd not been so deep in the depths of complete despair, I may have actually listened to it.

> The fear-based-thinking monster can always rear its big, ugly head – it's the job of your Higher Self not to listen to it.

My first big question centred on what business leaders deemed the ideal conditions for setting up some sort of business on your own to be. Google was my only research tool and it quickly became clear there are *no* ideal conditions to start a business. Sure, there are favourable conditions, but never ideal.

Here's a small selection of the encouraging gems I was mentally battling:

- Single parents don't do this
- It's financially precarious
- What if I fail?
- Massive assumption people will want to work with me over another PR consultancy
- There are a lot of very well-established, excellent PR consultancies
- I'm sleep-deprived
- Two precious little people are relying on me
- This is not the time for risk-taking
- You're delusional
- It will never work.

As I had no money, I didn't have the luxury of time to sit, ponder and really think about whether this was the best option. I'm really glad time was limited because I play it safe by nature; I don't take risks. You won't see me jumping out of planes or bungee jumping, ever. Even exploring this thought was a big risk, so a lack of time was a blessing of gigantic proportions. There wasn't time to dither and contemplate; I had mouths to feed. Nate was just two months old, Luca was three; they were completely dependent on me and would be for quite some time. My heart kept whispering, then shouting, 'Do it; it just feels right. *Do it, Lisa. Do it!*'

When the decision had to be made, because quite frankly I had to earn money and fast, I turned to my favourite book of all time, *The Alchemist* by Paulo Coelho. I metaphorically placed myself firmly in the shoes of the main character. I was the boy, Santiago, in this moment in my life; stuck between my flock and my treasure. I had to choose between something I had become accustomed to, and something I wanted to have.

The flock was safe and made practical sense, but it'd always be there. I knew fortune favoured the brave.

At that moment in time, when everything else had been stripped away, I decided that I wanted the treasure.

---

The flock is safe and practical, but it'll always be there. Fortune favours the brave – so do you *really* want the treasure?

---

## Pros & Cons List

If you're on the fence with an idea or a decision, this simple list-making exercise can bring more clarity than any conversation, psychic reading or Google search ever will. Think of something you can feel inside you that you want to do - a little dream bubbling away in your belly.

Now, take ten minutes to list below all the reasons why you should go for it (the pros) and all the reasons you believe you shouldn't (the cons). I promise you that this quick process will deliver you the guidance you're seeking.

Always remember that more cons than pros doesn't mean it's a bad idea and you shouldn't go for it - my list showed only *one* pro, but by writing all my thoughts down in my own handwriting, I knew what the answer was. Note: being 'scared' or 'it won't work' don't count as cons, in any situation!

# DREAM A LITTLE DREAM

## *PROs + CONs TEMPLATE*

**PROs** (why I should go for it)      **CONs** (why I should leave it)

_____    _____

_____    _____

_____    _____

_____    _____

_____    _____

_____    _____

_____    _____

_____    _____

_____    _____

_____    _____

_____    _____

_____    _____

_____    _____

_____    _____

_____    _____

# 02

# Feeling

# the fear

## (and doing it anyway)

I was undoubtedly in a state of flow when I made the decision to work for myself. If you've ever experienced what I'm referring to, you'll know what I mean when I write that it all makes sense once you stop fighting against it and accept the path laid before you.

I was going to set up something on my own, allowing myself six months to make a go of it and get to a financially stable position. If it didn't work, I'd apply for other jobs and put it down to experience. The relief of putting a stake in the ground was enormous! After months of floating and grappling with a total lack of self-worth, I had a goal!

Off I went, scared out of my mind I'd fail but filled with hope that maybe, just maybe, I wouldn't.

---

## LITTLE DREAM: To have my own business so I can always be there for my boys

---

Working for myself and building the start of a business was very much like building a house, as I discovered later on, when I did in fact build a house. I was putting in place the basic structures: a solid framework from which to grow. Oh, and I had no idea what I was doing. I might as well have been building an actual house, with the lack of knowledge I had!

Thankfully, I'd had a bird's-eye view of running a PR consultancy from some of the best in the business, both in the UK and Australia. Of course, once you're in the hot seat, there are all manner of things to deal with that you'll never be privy to as an employee. But I had an insight at least and that helped enormously. I'm also a doer by nature, a very favourable thing to be at this point.

Once I decided I was setting up a business, my parents funded the purchase of a basic laptop and I did some online research about what to do next. 'How do I start a business?' went into the Google search bar and up popped heaps of information about different structures and where to go to make it happen. I set up a sole trader ABN (Australian Business Number), which took all of twenty minutes. In my head and heart, this made me legit.

I also registered a business name with ASIC (Australian Securities and Investments Commission): again, a quick Google search showed a raft of websites set up to help do this quickly. My trading name was decided in about two minutes flat - no fancy workshops or brand exploration sessions took place. I wanted something short that was linked to me, and that did what it said on the tin. I didn't expect this 'being my own boss' thing would last beyond six months anyway so it didn't matter what I called it. LBPR was available and that's what I went with.

I had an ABN, a registered business name and a laptop. If anyone who's seriously considering setting up a new business asks me what to do first, I will always list these three actions. If I had my time again, I'd add in getting a very good accountant, but for me at that time, my focus was on having some numbers to actually discuss with the accountant. A blank spreadsheet wouldn't have been that interesting for either of us.

I then turned my thoughts to a logo for LBPR because I needed some sort of visual identity. Remember, at this stage, in my head, I was non-committal although my heart was in, boots and all! I reached out to friends. Emily Brooks, my best friend from London, created a logo for me.

This was given to another beautiful friend in Kiama, Helen Denniss, who designed business cards, email signatures, promo fliers and social media artwork. I gave them both zero direction because I had no idea what I wanted; I just knew I had to create some sort of 'look'. Thank heavens these two souls were talented, could work to a minimal (or no) budget, and knew me well enough to create branding that worked for me at that time.

Finally, I enlisted the talent and camera of locally based photographer Phil Winterton to take some photos of me so I looked the part. He found us a million-dollar-plus place in Kiama to use for a few hours, and didn't I look like I had it together! I had to laugh later that night as I went to bed; Phil arrived to take photos and just ten minutes before I'd been covered in baby spew, with my hair and make-up yet to be sorted. The amazing photos he managed to capture of a dishevelled single mum that day are a testament to his ability!

The day I was ready to 'launch' – and by launch I mean tell people I was setting up my own PR offering and available to help from my kitchen table with a tracksuit on (no, it sadly wasn't a glass-clinking affair à la *Absolutely Fabulous*) – I felt an enormous sense of calm. I think that was for two reasons: I'd surrendered to the process, which somehow alleviated all expectation and pressure, and I had absolutely nothing to lose.

---

You will feel an enormous sense of calm once you surrender to the process ... this somehow alleviates all expectation and pressure, and you suddenly have absolutely nothing to lose.

---

The time from the moment I decided to go for it to this 'launch' was only a month. It was happening fast but it had to. I wanted to be off single parent benefits. I didn't want to have to ask Mum and Dad for money. I looked forward to buying whatever I wanted at the supermarket. When distilled down into a single thought, my little dream in that moment really was simply to be self-sufficient again.

On the day of the launch, as always, I dropped little Luca to Mum and Dad, got my coffee with Nate and headed home. That morning Nate slept soundly in his car seat, which was not the norm. I took that rare event as a sign that the universe had given me some time to send out the emails I'd drafted 100 times in my head; to hit 'yes' on the social media accounts (Facebook, Twitter and Instagram); to actually move the arrow on the dial from fiction to fact.

So, I did. I wrote my emails to all the people I could think of: friends, family, friends of friends, marketing and PR contacts. And then I hit send.

*Send, send, send.*

And that's the unglamorous moment when I said goodbye to: Lisa Burling. Single mum. Unemployed. And hello to: Lisa Burling. Single mum. Managing Director of LBPR.

## A little dream had come true.

I immediately received messages of encouragement and support. These weren't opportunities that would convert to paid work directly but, my goodness, did they fill up my confidence cup, which in turn propelled me forward and kept me going with my new business drive on the days I was sure I couldn't.

I had invitations to attend local networking groups where I met some amazing friends and supporters, and I started to share my skills and experience with potential clients who offered me small, but important, pieces of paid work. Yes, paid work!

Instagram paints a picture of potted plants, MacBook Pros and froth-art cappuccinos - commonly referred to as 'laptop lifestyles' - as the reality of an entrepreneur/small business owner. And you know what? For some people, I'm sure it is. For me, it was not. It was a kitchen table, dirty dishes in the sink, baby stuff everywhere and stolen moments between loads of washing, meal time, preschool, swimming lessons, paediatrician appointments and little sleep. Some nights, no sleep. I guess I can say categorically it is possible to build a business when in a constant state of jetlag, where the study sample size is one. I'd finally get to my own bed around midnight and each morning I'd wake up at ridiculous o'clock (4 am to be exact, never by choice). I was shattered all day and honestly grateful I didn't need to show up to an actual office with other well-dressed, hair-brushed humans every day.

Every phone call was taken with either a sleeping baby or a pile of dirty washing in one arm. Every proposal was written in fits and starts, very late at night. I became an expert at one-handed typing and I defy anybody to beat me at it. My brain was whizzing at a million miles an hour when it hit the pillow, listing all I hadn't done and all I needed to do.

If anyone was to have come to my home office in the early days – and I use the description 'home office' loosely, because it was actually the kitchen bench – they'd see a laptop with dried up milk on the keyboard, juice-stained papers all over the place, a baby on my knee while I balanced my mobile phone on my ear and a toddler singing along loudly to ABC Kids: 'We all know frogs go la de dah de dah'.

Because I felt socially and professionally isolated, I'd plan to meet at least one local businessperson for coffee each week, just so I had a reason to engage with the real world and put some decent clothes on. At those times, my mum would come over and watch Nate and Luca for me, so I could escape for an hour. Yes, escape.

One person I met with semi-regularly in those early days was a marketer called Kerry. She reached out to me early on as she needed a PR consultant to help with a project. I've only recently told her how instrumental to my wellbeing our coffee catch-ups were. She was a supporter from day one and I am eternally grateful to her for believing in me.

I learnt the hard way that small business in particular is not for those who need consistency and structure to be happy. Think of it like the arcade game where you're constantly hitting a mole on the head with a hammer: as one goes down and disappears, two more pop up.

I really can't describe it any better than that, except to say I came to always expect the unexpected.

In the back of my head this entire time, all I could hear was a nagging voice saying: 'Just take a job Lisa, make it easier on yourself.' To ignore this voice was very hard, especially when I was trying to appease a small baby with a dummy while advising a client on the best media strategy for their new product launch. In those first few months, I was truly overwhelmed. I was so tired; I'd heard people say they were 'bone-tired' before and now I knew what it actually meant.

I was firmly in survival mode but, no matter what was thrown at me, I had to make it work. I'd chosen Option B and it had to deliver in just six months. But it was a constant juggle and so freaking hard that I almost threw in the towel at least twice a week. Why didn't I actually throw it in? Because I just *knew* I was onto something. Because I didn't want to give up and I knew this little dream would help me realise some others I had percolating away if I stuck at it. I knew in my heart this was a little dream worth sticking at.

---

## Don't give up, especially when you feel like it's your only option! Every little dream will help you realise some others if you stick at it.

---

Despite being a team of one, despite living well outside of the Big Smoke, despite being sleep deprived and feeling like I was having an out-of-body experience every single day, I was still a PR professional with significant global experience, a journalism degree and a natural ability to connect with other humans. I was still me.

I pushed through the reasons not to, did the work every day, believed in me and there it was. I never, ever allowed myself to forget that, despite all the hard work and times of feeling overwhelmed, my little dream was actually happening.

As hard as it was, I was still doing it, and that counted for a lot.

## How Can This Work for You?

You may be thinking 'Well, of course setting up a PR consultancy was working for you; you had experience and contacts so the chances of success were higher.' And you know what? That is completely true. I'd never recommend that someone in my situation go forward with a business proposition where you have zero experience, no contacts, and possibly no market. The moral is that all of us - you, me, your aunty, neighbour, whoever it may be - have a toolkit of people and talents and experience that may have the ability to pull you out of an almighty big dark hole. Employment or lack thereof is just one of life's curve balls, and there are many others. I just know that the DNA of a little dream will guide you every single time as to what you go for now, and what to come back to at a later date. Your future self will most definitely thank you for the gumption you apply to making changes and taking action right now.

## Are Little Dreams Masculine or Feminine Energy?

For the record, we all have masculine and feminine energy and it has nothing to do with whether you're a male or female. I took an online test that leading mindset guru and life coach Tony Robbins has on his website to see what my dominant energy is and, surprise, surprise, it's masculine!

As Tony notes, the masculine energy focuses on one task or issue at a time and is about total focus, achieving the goal that has been set. It's all about doing - analytical, impatient, assertive and logical. The feminine energy on the other hand is about being and can involve taking in everything at once; it's softer and goes with the flow, focusing on the greater good rather than the nitty-gritty details.

It's tempting to see little dreams as purely feminine energy because they sound so floaty and lovely, but they are almost entirely rooted in masculine energy. Gumption is surely the core definition of it!

Of course, if your dominant energy is feminine, this doesn't mean you can't make little dreams come true. It just may mean you have to learn to apply masculine thinking to it a little more consciously.

Try Tony's test for yourself here: **https://core.tonyrobbins.com/ gender-quotient-4/**

# 03

Money

matters...

when
you have

American founding father, the principal author of the Declaration of Independence and the third president of the United States Thomas Jefferson famously said, 'Never spend your money before you have it.'

Luckily for me, that wasn't a choice I had to make. LBPR started with no money. Bank balance: $0. Money set aside to invest in business: $0.

I knew my business had to start earning money, and fast. There was no nest egg, no trust fund, no little pot I could dip into. Any money I had was via Centrelink or a little cash injection from the Bank of Mum and Dad. I detested the fact I was on 'benefits'; I detested that I used what we call in Australia a Pension Card to get a cheaper rate on the renewal of my driver's licence. If any situation needed a little dream to make it better, this was it.

## LITTLE DREAM: To stop single parent benefits and earn a proper income

When I dared to think slightly longer term, I dreamt a little dream that saw me turn this single income into a sustainable business model, while mitigating the risk of losing everything. But I wasn't there yet. 'Dream small Lisa, stay focused,' whispered my heart.

One particular person, who is now a good friend and remains one of LBPR's biggest clients, rang me as I was standing in my kitchen feeling the self-doubt kick in. She said she had some new brands to launch, and she remembered me from a new business presentation a few years earlier. She wondered if I'd be up for working with her on this project, 'Even though the budget is small. I only have $10,000.'

I was standing in my kitchen, looking out at the street and all was quiet. Luca was playing Duplo in his cubbyhouse and Nate was asleep. That's right, it was such a pivotal moment in the timeline of my new life that I remember *exactly* where we all were and what we were doing. I started to cry. I was so grateful for this woman I barely knew who believed in me so much more than I did. I managed to hold back the full-body sobs and get through the rest of the conversation with my professional veneer intact: 'I'm sure we can do something with that budget. If you send me a brief, I'll pull together some ideas for you to consider.'

Not long after this, my first purchase order came through. That changed everything. I had proper money coming in! Now, I was literally in business. I set up a Microsoft Excel spreadsheet and entered $10,000 into a column titled 'Incoming'. I detest Excel but that was without a doubt one of the most pleasurable moments of my life up to that point.

Scarily, this happened literally a week before the six-month deadline I'd set myself. I was only one week away from shutting the virtual doors, not just on LBPR, but also on all the magical experiences that I didn't know were yet to come.

After this, I was always on the lookout for clients that could offer ongoing work, with a steady monthly income. I preferred those that operated on a purchase order system too. This formal process of appointment always gave me the peace of mind that I'd get paid.

Thankfully, these clients kept coming to me: I delivered high quality work at a competitive price point, two very basic principles of business I inherently knew. My clients also referred me to other businesses that could offer ongoing work. PR is what others say about you and I was thrilled the DNA of my business-offering was now delivering amazing clients back to me.

As I acquired new clients, my love-hate Excel spreadsheet became a whole lot more interesting. I was paying myself a really low salary as I figured the profit was mine too, so as long as I had enough to live on, I was happy. I decided it was time to get professional. I called my friend Suzanne Haddon, a global specialist in brand identity. I asked if she would design a grown-up brand identity for my business.

I also realised that I had to get to Centrelink. This time, I simply couldn't wait to get there. As it turned out, the ticket system directed me to sit directly opposite the same man I'd wept in front of just six short months ago.

'You're back,' he said.

'I am. And I'm ready to stop my single parent benefits.'

'Wow. OK. That's great news.' Big smile from both of us.

'See? I told you. A helping hand. Congratulations, Lisa.'

I walked out of that place a foot taller and a whole heap lighter in my head, but especially in my heart. I walked across the road and sat down on the same park bench I'd cried at just six months earlier. I pulled out my phone my parents were no longer paying for and wouldn't you know it: a diary date popped up.

It was 29 July 2014.

'See? I told you things would get better!'

And so they had.

**A little dream had come true.**

## INVESTING IN YOUR FINANCES

I am all up for trying new things and upskilling myself in areas where I know very little and should know more. However, I firmly believe finance and accounting is no place for the novice to play, especially when it concerns a change in your personal financial situation, or money for a business.

I relied very heavily on my accountant and bookkeeper to guide me on financial decisions in the early days; they were, and still are, my trusted advisors for all aspects of my finances. I firmly believe outsourcing what you're no good at is critical to business success. I could have lost far more money than I paid my accountant if I did it myself; anyone who works with me knows I have only one skill in financial matters and that's undoing formulas in spreadsheets.

There are so many financial obligations to fulfil as a business owner in Australia (as I'm sure there are in other countries too!), including quarterly Business Activity Statements (BAS) that it really does pay to pay someone who knows what they're doing.

Choose an accountant who specialises in small business and understands what you need – and what you don't. For me, it's a profit and loss statement, and a forward projection spreadsheet showing what's going out in expenses and therefore what I need to bring in each month. The accounting software XERO is well worth the investment, before you get to a point where your incomings and outgoings are hard to keep track of and your BAS is a mess (yes, I am speaking from experience).

Also consider additional expenses and plan for them. For example, if you earn over a certain amount of money, you do need to collect GST (Goods & Services Tax) on behalf of the government; if you employ people, you need to take into account tax and superannuation. To ensure I'm never caught short, I have a separate bank account I transfer a generous amount of money into each month for these expenses (yes, once again, I am speaking from experience).

Think about your little dreams: are they going to cost you money before you make any? That can be OK, but it is a balancing act that must be carefully considered. I strongly advise you to discuss your plans (heck, just call them little dreams, it's always fun to make someone smile!) with someone who can advise on the financial validity of what you're hoping to do. This will save you a tonne of sleepless nights down the track and ensure you stay on track, applying your gumption to the ideas most likely to achieve your little dreams.

Not celebrating your SUCCESSES along the way is like building a house and not LIVING in it. What a waste of all that GUMPTION! Always take time to RECOGNISE what you've ACHIEVED – this is the very essence of DREAMING LITTLE.

# 04

# From the trenches

# TO
# A
# TEAM

Whether it's changing your employer or setting up a new business like I did, there's no doubt that any alteration in your career or job (or both!) consumes your thoughts. And if you're feeling stuck in a rut and you know you need to make a change to ensure your own happiness, people who love and care for you can offer advice and support, but you're the one who has to make changes happen.

Rebuilding your professional life from the ground up can be a lonely existence in terms of your emotional and mental needs. Let me demonstrate my point. When I started my business and decided to work for myself, I realised that there was a lot of pressure on me, from me. I could never be 'off duty' and, even if I were to someday have a team around, the fact is, the buck stopped with me.

I spent the first six months of LBPR's existence doing it all on my own. You name it, I did it. Yes, I was very tired and my to-do list was ridiculously long but I I'm grateful that I had to go backwards – doing many tasks I did as a junior PR – to move LBPR forward. As a result of being firmly back in the trenches, I can say that I know every element of my business intimately, every process and procedure, because I created and implemented them myself. I knew the names of key journalists, the shifts in the industry that I needed to be aware of (my social media DIY lessons where I taught myself how it all worked have proven to be invaluable today). Even to this day, I love getting in and doing the work; I never aspired to be a business owner, but I always wanted to be surrounded by words and people who loved the power of effective communication as much as I did.

From writing work-in-progress documents, keeping track of the (limited) cash flow, being the primary client contact, calling journalists, writing new business proposals and evaluation reports, and overseeing a very fluid marketing plan for LBPR (basically, I made the marketing up as a I went along!), I was the entire C-suite - CEO, COO, CMO and CFO - all rolled into one neat (and very tired) little package.

Excitingly but also a little scarily, less than one year into LBPR's journey, I faced a big decision. (This, dear reader, is something to bear in mind as you embark on your own little dream adventure. Decisions are constantly there, exactly like a Choose Your Own Adventure book. It's never a 'set and forget' situation when you're making things happen fast, and you need to trust your own judgement – yes, that trusty gut feel – at all times as to the best next move). I either needed to find someone to work with me or start turning down work. It's a fact that time is finite; there are only so many hours in the day. If you're an accountant, a lawyer, or anyone in a service-based business where the primary commodity is people, you will understand the challenges that come with selling what is in essence an intangible resource. So, to build a successful business where you sell time, it stands to reason that there comes a point where the work you need to do outweighs the time you have available.

It's a critical juncture where these two variables – time available versus work on offer – meet, because you're essentially deciding whether you want to grip your knickers and get bigger, be a sole trader or a company. Yes, I could have worked with external contractors and freelancers, but by this point I felt a little lonely and was eager to have a sidekick – a Robin to my Batman, if you will.

As requests from potential clients started to increase, I knew I'd have to start saying no. Quality wasn't something I was willing to compromise, and that's the first thing that goes when you're tired and overstretched. The other option was to take on someone to work with me. So, of course, me being me – in for a penny, in for a pound, as the saying goes – I decided to take on an employee. I'd recently moved into an apartment in the centre of Wollongong with my boys and, if they shared a bedroom, we could use the other as LBPR's HQ.

## LITTLE DREAM:
### To have an employee to help me at LBPR.

As with any little dream, I had to start somewhere. Somewhere can be as simple as an online search, and so for me I started out by researching what a junior PR salary looked like with the Public Relations Institute of Australia to make sure what I could offer was fair and competitive. Yes, step one of a little dream can simply be a few clicks on a mouse! I also knew what junior consultants had been paid at previous employers. There is a misconception that people are paid less outside of Australian capital cities like Sydney and Melbourne, and that is not the case at LBPR (we are based in Wollongong, an hour south of Sydney). I wanted, and still want, the best PR consultants available because talented people are passionate, work fast and deliver amazing quality work. My dad said to me once, 'You pay peanuts, you get monkeys, Blossy!' and he's spot on!

My accountant and I crunched the numbers and, to my disbelief, I was more than ready financially to take on a paid helper, offering a good salary. I was hesitant to advertise the role, as I simply didn't have time to sift through resumes and conduct multiple interviews. I trusted this person was seeking me just as I was seeking them: that if I put it out there and started talking about it, someone just perfect would arrive.

As it turns out, that's exactly what happened.

My first employee came to me through a conversation with a friend who introduced me to the PR Major Co-ordinator at the University of Wollongong. I told her I was really busy and was looking for a stellar performer to join my growing business. 'I think I know the perfect person,' she said and within two days I'd met this person and the decision was made. It was a yes, from both of us!

After my first day of working together with my new employee, once the boys were asleep, I sat with my cup of tea in the 'office' (I'm a sucker for an English Breakfast tea at the end of the day) and I giggled –not because it was funny, but because it was amazing! The world truly is a magical place when you set your intention and believe it can happen. Through my consistent hard work and constant visualisation of my little dream, I now had someone else who saw my vision and wanted to work with *me*. Yes, I felt a bit overwhelmed but I knew if I kept my little dreams in order, the gratitude swelling in my heart would inevitably catch up.

> 'The world truly is a magical place when you set your intention and believe it can happen. Through consistent hard work and constant visualisation of your little dream, you'll draw others to you who see your vision and want it to come true, too.'

We'd work solidly in a very small room with our desks facing each other. Luca and Nate were at preschool by then so I could still fulfil my dream to be there for them, as I had help if I needed it. The volume of work we got through still amazes me, thanks in no small part to our big pieces of butcher's paper stuck with Blu-Tack to the mirrored in-built cupboards! I have so much fondness for those early days where LBPR firmly transitioned into a more grown-up business.

Building a team was a big moment for me, happening much sooner than I thought it would, because I chunked it down and dreamed small.

## A little dream had come true.

Not long after I took on my first employee, it became evident through the sheer volume of work and a healthy balance sheet that I needed to employ another staff member. This was really exciting as I was truly creating a team, a vision I'd had for a few years down the track that was happening now! It took me a while to commit to having two people who relied on LBPR for their income; I always looked after me first as I wasn't ever going back to single parent benefits. But I wasn't able to work a full eight-hour day as I wanted to be there for my boys after they finished preschool, so I knew having two trusted people to help keep the momentum going for our clients was a wise move for not only my little dreams for this business I was developing, but also the little dreams I had around being a great, present mum to my sons.

When I did finally see that having two employees wasn't a choice but a necessity for my own sanity and for my other extremely important role as a mum, the timely delivery of client work and the future growth of LBPR, I got excited about it. At this time, as if by magic yet again, my IT consultant introduced me to a PR graduate looking for a part-time role. We had a coffee, and within thirty minutes she was in the office working away!

Of course, this growth in my team meant I was no longer able to operate the business without a professional office space. We needed somewhere that reflected where we were but, more importantly, where we were going.

## LITTLE DREAM:
### To have a professional office for LBPR.

My Google research in the early days revealed to me that the two biggest expenses for any small business are staff and rent, and I was really hesitant about paying rent for somewhere that would put financial pressure on me. I had been on single parent benefits just over twelve months earlier, living at home with Mum and Dad, and I didn't want to feel that way again, ever. Simultaneously, I recognised team productivity was reliant on providing the right workplace environment. My next little dream was upon me.

When I was running my business from a kitchen table, my reality just twelve months earlier, I'd dream of having a proper office. Now, here I was, in a position to make it come true! I ran the numbers with my accountant, and we could afford up to A$500 per week for an office space – including rent and other expenses like electricity and internet. To be honest, the fact I had this amount available to me for an office, after salaries and other business expenses like electricity and insurances were taken into account, surprised me. I know entrepreneurial reality TV shows like *Shark Tank* urge you to 'know your numbers' as a business grows, but I didn't know my numbers at this point other than that I was sending out invoices as payment for quality work. I focused on the work, not the dollars, and the result was a financially healthy business that exceeded any expectations I had at that time.

After much searching, we found a space offering all we needed for a reasonable price. I only signed a one-year lease (and it was good I did, as one year after that we needed somewhere bigger, which is where LBPR is now).

I won't lie; it took some time for me to adjust to this little dream coming true. Just a small word of caution here: when little dreams come true thick and fast, you can forget to breathe and enjoy the moment. It's so easy, no matter what little dream we are focusing on, to get carried away on the seas of momentum, and you'll notice people are almost encouraging you to keep up the pace you've set. (As an aside, this is exactly why my least favourite question is 'So, what's next?'; it steals the joy of what's now.) The fundamental problem with not stopping and putting the anchor down to just bob up and down on the waves is that we will inevitably end up seasick and unsure of the best direction to take. Little dreams are all about celebrating the goals you kick on your way to the big dream, and I forgot to do that several times. Consider this a polite warning from an old hand at this little dream stuff.

*Just a small word of caution here – when little dreams come true thick and fast, you can forget to breathe and enjoy the moment.
Stop and acknowledge what you've done!
From little things, big things grow.*

After our first week in the new space, I vividly remember taking time to be alone there, on a weekend when my boys were with their dad. It was totally quiet and the lights were off. I sat at my desk and remembered the days in Kiama at the kitchen bench: the makeshift office in my apartment. This evolution had all happened in just twelve months! I felt so much nostalgia and heartfelt thanks. For the first time since this crazy ride started, I was finally ready to give myself a pat on the back.

## A little dream had come true.

Jim Collins, the author of famous business book, *From Good to Great*, devotes an entire section to the importance of getting the right people on the bus. This can mean hiring someone even when you don't have a role yet … so strong is his belief that a good cultural fit is paramount to success in the business world. I totally support this view and believe it's especially true when you have a small team - nobody can hide and any disharmony needs to be dealt with immediately.

I assess a person's 'vibe' when I'm hiring someone. What do I mean by that? Well, if you are qualified and have relevant experience, that's important, but if my gut tells me you're a good operator with aligned values and a positive disposition, it's almost impossible for me not to hire you if there's a suitable position available.

I have only advertised a role at LBPR once; by luck or sheer clarity of my little dreams, the right people have found me at the right time. It's been a lovely process getting to know someone and assessing their suitability for my business.

---

When you're focused on making little dreams come true, the right people will find you at the right time. They'll have a strong sense of where you're going and want to be a part of the ride.

---

The only stumbling block I've experienced was when I was advised to hire a PA; it's the only role for which I've advertised and it's telling it didn't work out. Being introduced to potential staff via a trusted source, or getting to know someone over a number of informal meetings, is very different to a formal interview process where, let's be honest, nobody is themselves (interviewer included). I'll also admit the work for a PA at LBPR is minimal, mainly because I am so damned organised. In retrospect, it wasn't going to work out regardless of how I recruited for it.

My team sees LBPR as a business they can play a fundamental role in shaping: if anyone has an idea, I want to know about it and see how we can make it work, as long as it adds value. We don't have headcounts that say someone can't be promoted or that we can't employ new people; there's a strong sense of where we are going and a desire to be a part of the ride.

I know my team value me and understand the journey I've been on to get to a point where I can not only pay myself, but them too. Some days, when I am at my desk in our beautiful office, I'll appear to be glancing around deep in thought; but really, I am pinching myself that I am surrounded by talented people who spend their days building their career with me. I still get an enormous thrill when I hear one of them say on the phone they're from LBPR, or see that they've updated their social media profile to display the fact they work with me.

I always take it as a massive compliment that, of all the businesses in my field, in the whole world, some of the most talented PR professionals I've ever worked with chose LBPR and me.

With any little dream that requires the input of others like staff, a specific skillset or contact (tip: all the ones worth pursuing do need help from the outside world), it's a good idea to consider who you're recruiting to help you and why. Don't ever feel obligated to bring someone in on your little dream – confide in, work with, court those that are proud to see you succeed and who are genuinely invested in your life being the very best it can be. You'll know a little dreamer when you see them – they're the ones with gumption. Every. Single. Time.

## THOUGHT SPARK: THE VALUE OF PROFESSIONAL VALUES

When I worked in London at a phenomenal healthcare PR consultancy called Virgo HEALTH, under the amazing leadership of PR industry leaders Angie Wiles and Sarah Matthew, I saw firsthand how fundamental values were to the success as a business. Every team member lived and breathed the values and as a result, the business was hugely successful.

Around the walls of LBPR's HQ you'll see our values proudly displayed: Stumble Don't Fall, Perspective. Always, Stand Together, Exude Passion, Constantly Wow, Substance Over Flash, Pursue Growth and Embrace Change.

The truth is, I came up with LBPR's values all by myself, early on in the journey when it was just little old me. Even if LBPR never grew beyond me, I still wanted to ensure there was a compass that could guide decisions and help navigate the inevitable highs and lows of small business and consultancy life.

So, how do you come up with values? I know businesses that've brought in an external consultant to help the team drill down into the essence of what the business stands for. I also know businesses that did what I did. Personally, I believe the business owner knows what they are and, as the consistent team member, this content should flow from the top down. Start with a list that your team can help you flesh out into tangible statements. It's one thing to have 'be energetic' as a value, but quite another to uphold it as part of your daily work if you don't know what 'being energetic' actually means in real terms.

Of course, it's one thing to have values but the important part is to use them! LBPR's values are my guide to employing team members and each value has a set of behaviours I do - and don't - want to see. Demonstrating our values forms part of everyone's professional development plan too.

## LBPR Values

Here are some examples of how LBPR's values distil into the way our team behaves (there are up to five do and don't behaviours for each value so I am just sharing a sample here):

### Stumble Don't Fall

**Do:** See challenges as opportunities to grow from

**Don't:** Let an issue become much bigger than it actually is

Perspective. Always

**Do:** Seek input of team members - a problem shared is a problem halved

**Don't:** Allow emotions to override common sense and rational thought

### Stand Together

**Do:** Take a collaborative approach to all we do

**Don't:** Not offer to step in and help a team member in need of advice and support

### *Exude Passion*

**Do:** Always give it your all

**Don't:** Lack momentum towards the vision and mission

### *Constantly Wow*

**Do:** Think outside the box to add true value

**Don't:** Adopt a 'that'll do' mindset

### *Substance Over Flash*

**Do:** Create client strategies that work

**Don't:** Use tactical thinking not backed by strategic thought

### *Pursue Growth*

**Do:** Proactively take on challenges – never say no, and don't wait to be asked!

**Don't:** Resist opportunities to step outside your 'comfort zone'

### *Embrace Change*

**Do:** Be flexible and adaptable

**Don't:** Put up a 'brick wall' and be close-minded.

## WHAT ARE YOUR PROFESSIONAL VALUES?

_____

_____

_____

_____

_____

_____

## DO THEY ALIGN WITH YOUR EMPLOYER?

_____

_____

_____

## IF YOU RUN YOUR OWN BUSINESS, DO YOU HAVE
## PROFESSIONAL VALUES?

_____

_____

_____

## DO YOU LIVE AND BREATHE THESE VALUES?

_____

_____

_____

Trust me, some time spent now on this will reap significant benefits in the future!

Do it now, so your little dreams can come true!

# 05

# AN ACCIDENTAL INNOVATION

I've heard it said that creativity is *thinking up* new things, whereas innovation is *doing* new things. I'm a doer, and that's how an innovation I hadn't seen as one came to be.

**W**ith a few little dreams coming true at record speed, due to a tonne of hard work and gumption, my business was now in a secure place with solid clients, a dedicated team and a fantastic office space. I now had room to *think* about new things, which for me centred on ways I could give back. It took me a while to grasp that I had reached this point so quickly, but hey, that's the true power of dreaming little. Once you chunk down the elephant, you can eat it a lot faster.

---

That's the true power of dreaming little. Once you chunk down the elephant, you can eat it a lot faster.

---

From LBPR's inception, we'd provided pro bono support to my cousin's charity, the Trish Multiple Sclerosis Research Foundation (please visit **www.trishmsresearch.org.au** to find out more) and I wanted to do more to give back. It was always my unarticulated intention at some point down the track to launch an initiative that fulfilled my desire to see charities access quality PR counsel for free and, in tandem, to nurture junior PR talent.

The University of Wollongong started asking me to guest lecture each semester on topics that could show students what PR in the real world looked like: media relations, working with digital influencers, social media strategy and issues preparedness and management, to name just a few areas I've presented on to PR students (and continue to now). I observed the students were great at communications and PR theory, because they were being fed this in bucket loads. However, the reality of life as a PR professional wasn't allowed for in the curriculum quite as much as I felt it should be.

I was sure that, if I applied the DNA of a little dream to this situation with a healthy serving of gumption, I could come up with a way to address these two challenges simultaneously: talented degree-qualified PR graduates not getting enough real-life experience before entering the PR industry, and charities not getting their important messages out to raise vital funds, due to lack of staff capabilities and funds to employ professional PR services. A lovely side benefit for LBPR was the opportunity to identify PR talent before they left tertiary education and offer the best graduates a job, based on observing them in a real-life situation.

This little dream was a three-pronged one all about innovation; it required significant action. There was no doubt I needed to *do* a lot of new things to make it happen.

---

LITTLE DREAM: To create a new initiative that could help charities access PR for free, give PR students real life experience *and* help me identify star talent early for LBPR.

---

I thought on this little dream for a few months before I took action and verbalised it to anyone – much longer than the little dreams that had come before. This was because it wasn't a necessity. I recognised this one was a 'nice to have', not a must-do. I was acutely aware it had the very real potential to overstretch me in terms of my time; my sons remained my priority, as did making money to live on.

Put simply, if I was going to spend time on this little dream, I had to ensure it wasn't going to jeopardise another, namely my first little dream, which you'll remember was to build my own business so I could be there for my boys. Herein lies an important little dream lesson and another gentle reminder: sometimes they stack up so fast (because you're a doer and they like that) that they can jeopardise each other coming to fruition. Just like the air traffic controller at a busy airport, you must know when it's their time to land because, let's face it, there's only so much room on the runway.

This is an important little dream lesson; sometimes they stack up so fast (because you're a doer and they like that) that they can jeopardise each other coming to fruition. Just like the air traffic controller at a busy airport, you must know when it's each little dream's time to land because, let's face it, there's only so much room on the runway.

Of course, I also had a big fear it might flop and, after coming so far, I wasn't sure I was ready for that. Then again, when are you ever ready for a flop?

After careful consideration, with my two team members working well and my boys actually sleeping and in bed by 6 pm most nights (oh, how I miss those days!), I found I had about an hour at night to map out what this could look like in tangible terms - so, roughly five hours a week.

In my mind's eye, this concept was essentially an internship on steroids - there were no cups of tea to be made. With their own desks and their own clients, the students would receive true hands-on experience before officially entering the PR industry. In essence, this was a catalyst for students to truly experience the real world of PR before they entered the industry, and for charities to see the benefit PR can bring to their profile and fundraising efforts. So that's what it was called: the Catalyst Student PR Consultancy, powered by LBPR and backed by the University of Wollongong.

That was the easy part. Now, the hard work started! It was not a straightforward process to get this little dream off the ground and had I known what lay ahead, I may have filed it away under 'A' for 'Another Time'.

> Don't expect all your little dreams to be quick, easy wins; little doesn't mean straightforward. Always remember: every small step is leading you towards something amazing. Hold on to the essence of your little dream. Keep going.

What ensued was a real David and Goliath battle between bureaucracy and a nimble start-up. There were phone calls, Skype calls, discussion documents and emails, and plenty of moments when I questioned why I was doing this when I *really* didn't have the time and it wasn't making me any money directly. But through the challenges, I could see the benefits that would come from the end result. I always held onto the essence of my bigger dream, so I kept going.

Not long after this 'what am I doing?' moment, I experienced what I believe was a God wink (this is what I call moments where I know I'm onto something). It was on a Skype call with the Public Relations Institute of Australia (PRIA). We wanted PRIA's endorsement of Catalyst and to see if they knew of any similar initiatives. What happened next was mind-blowing. After that call, we found out that, not only would PRIA endorse Catalyst, but that it was an Australian first and quite possibly a global first!

The then CEO, Graham Le Roux commented at the time, 'When we first heard about Catalyst we were delighted; this innovation is exactly what the public relations and communication industry needs. It is fabulous for the industry to have such creative thinkers out there like Lisa. The initiative is leading the way for the public relations and communications industry not just in Australia but across world and we know the program is only getting started.'

Julian Kenny, National Education Manager at the time, who supported the idea immediately and helped us enormously, said, 'Innovation in the field of education is something that, in managing the PRIA university accreditation program, I was happy to recognise. Catalyst is Australia's first student-run consultancy, and Lisa's initiative will transform classroom knowledge into real-life PR competencies and I believe other education providers will soon follow her ground-breaking lead.'

That was it. It was full steam ahead! Within a week, we had a logo, I'd rearranged LBPR's office to give the students a proper space, and there was a call out on LBPR's social media seeking charitable organisations to participate. The internship team at the University of Wollongong sought out their best final year PR students to be part of the initial Catalyst intake. The local media covered the story and this led to a waiting list of both students and charities needing help in this way. I even made the front cover of PRIA's magazine: the first and last time I expect to grace the front cover of a magazine with my 5-foot-2-inch frame!

On 10 February 2016, LBPR's Catalyst Student Consultancy was officially launched, in collaboration with the University of Wollongong. One of our first Catalyst interns said her experience allowed her to put theory into practice and was an invaluable part of building her skills in the field in conjunction with her studies. This feedback made my heart sing!

Since its launch, the LBPR Catalyst student PR consultancy has assisted six amazing charities – SCARF, Care & Share for Autism, the Trish MS Research Foundation, Need A Feed, The Kindness Project, and Saving Chloe Saxby. They have all benefited from free PR delivered by University of Wollongong students in LBPR's Catalyst Student Consultancy.

Considering I had been flat broke and on Centrelink single parent benefits less than two years previously, realising this little dream was a big moment for me. To be able to give back to charities that needed help, and the PR industry, when just a short time earlier I had literally nothing to give, remains one of my proudest moments of my life.

'Fortune favours the brave' is my go-to quote and it rang especially true with the realisation of LBPR's Catalyst Student Consultancy.

## Another little dream had come true.

In retrospect, the Catalyst Student Consultancy was a great concept but I failed to recognise it as a little dream that perhaps presented itself to me far too early. As Elizabeth Gilbert, the author of *Eat Pray Love* says in one of her subsequent books called *Big Magic,* ideas are always floating about our heads waiting for one of us to claim them before another human does. I became a little panicky that, if I didn't take this idea and action it with my little dream philosophy immediately, someone else would do it. So, I claimed the idea and went hell for leather, while I had a parallel little dream track for my core business, and a nearby little dream branch line for my role as mum. This was too much and it did end up making me very unwell (as you'll go on to read).

Once you start to list your little dreams (and trust me, they will flow out of your head and heart at record speed once you get into the zone!), it's a good idea to prioritise and be ruthless at filing away those that sound fun but actually aren't going to do what they're meant to do for you - change your life right now for the better, and fast. I have a journal filled with little dreams that are yet to come to life, as I finally realised that by simply writing them down, I am tethering the idea to me in some way, just as Elizabeth Gilbert suggests in her book. I have reconciled that some of the little dreams may not actually come true and that's totally OK. There's more than enough on the go to keep me out of trouble.

## ALL IT TAKES IS A LITTLE GUMPTION ... STEPS TO TAKE NOW

I do hope after reading about my personal experiences in Part 1 you can see the enormous benefits being brave can bring you and that you're inspired to give it a go!

My journey shows you that life is exactly that: a journey. I had no aspirations to be a business owner until life changed and it became an option worth exploring. I then dreamt little dreams, consistently worked towards them, was always brave; and now? I'm one very content and proud owner of an award-winning PR consultancy, with an amazing team and phenomenal clients.

So, what are *your* little dreams when it comes to being brave about the way you approach your career and professional life? What can you do – just one little step – that takes some bravery but will take you from dull to dynamic in record speed? (Remember, you may have captured this at the start of the book too.)

Write down here what your little dream is when it comes to the professional side of you. Be as descriptive as you can and use the SMART framework – Specific, Measurable, Achievable, Realistic and Timebound – to make it tangible.

Maybe you want to leave your current job; maybe you want to introduce a new initiative that will make your time at work happier; maybe it's as a simple as actually taking a lunch break and getting that gym workout done.

To help you, here's what mine was at the start of the LBPR journey:

'My little dream is to work for myself for six months. I will set up an ABN, get a laptop and design my brand identity by February 2014; I will have three clients who pay me $2000 a month each by June 2014.'

Refer back to the DNA of a little dream at the start of this book if you need some clarity.

**MY LITTLE DREAM IS ...**

_____

_____

_____

**THIS LITTLE DREAM IS IMPORTANT TO ME BECAUSE ...**

_____

_____

_____

_____

**I NEED THESE PEOPLE OR RESOURCES TO HELP ME REALISE
THIS LITTLE DREAM ...**

_____

_____

_____

_____

Now you have your little dream captured, write down at least four steps you can take right now to make it come true. To help you, here's my task list linked to my first professional little dreams:

- Look at the Australian Business Register online and develop a shortlist of names I can share with my family and close friends; decide on the best one and register it!

- Purchase a laptop
- Make one call to a former client each week, asking if they have any upcoming projects
- Create a credentials document in PowerPoint telling my story, sharing my professional experience and showcasing four varied testimonials of actual campaigns I've worked on.

**MY LITTLE DREAM TASK LIST IS ...**

_____

_____

_____

_____

_____

I promise you this is how I started out - with a little dream and some actions. Seems simple, doesn't it? That's because it is!

You can repeat this exercise for as many little dreams as you like. There is no limit; however, I'd recommend keeping it to a maximum of six. Otherwise you run the risk of veering into big dream territory and that's where overwhelm and inertia are waiting to greet you.

# Dream small and keep moving. That's all you need to do to make it happen.

# PART 2

## Dreaming of ... BEING

## TRUE TO MYSELF

*You are not what they think of you*

# 06

# A SINGLE MUM ...

# WITH SWAGGER

J. K. Rowling once said, 'I am prouder of my years as a single mother than of any other part of my life.' I didn't understand what she meant when she said it, but I certainly do now.

**N**obody has 'single parent' on their vision board or written in their journal as a life goal. Yet being one gives me a lens to the reality of so many people I may not have otherwise understood; a front-row-seat insight into an existence that only comes from living it.

Setting up a business while raising children is madness, but doing it as a single parent is probably insanity. It's a constant juggling act and some days are complete chaos. It does help that I am a natural multitasker, have amazing parents, and am incredibly efficient. No human is an island and I ask for help when I need it.

One of the questions I get asked most is, 'How do you do it? How do you manage to raise your boys and meet all of their needs, and run your business, on your own?'

The CEO of Australia's largest community for women, Emma Isaacs, recently published her first book, *Winging It*. In it, she recounts being asked how she does it all; Emma is also mum to five children under the age of ten. She simply responds with the truth: 'I don't.'

Hear, hear Emma!

The truth is, I don't know anything different as a business owner. LBPR was set up so soon after Nate's arrival, caring for babies while simultaneously building a business has been my reality from day one. Luca and Nate also know no different. Luca once said to me as I was tapping away on my laptop, 'Mumma, are you saving the world?' It took all my strength not to burst into tears because, although I wasn't, and I'm still not saving the world, I was most definitely saving his, Nate's and mine at that point. I still am.

Once I was able to accept my new reality - Lisa Burling, single mum - and not burst into tears at the very thought of it, I knew I wanted to be an example to others in the same boat. Being a single parent is no impediment to achieving great things, one little dream at a time; in fact, in my experience, it has the potential to have quite the opposite effect.

> Proudly being who you are is no impediment to achieving great things, one little dream at a time; it has the potential to have quite the opposite effect.

Being a single parent doesn't mean my brain stops working; if anything, it had to, and continues to have to, work harder and faster. Being a single mum doesn't mean accepting a life of struggle, financially and emotionally. As I reminded myself daily back when my life was turned upside down, I was still myself and I still had lots to offer, right?

And, despite what the mass media feeds us, single parents are not a homogenous group. Sure, I started in the Centrelink queue signing up for single parent benefits, which is where the generalisations start, but I didn't stay there. Like all subgroups that society tries to define by a set of stereotypes, such as race, sexual orientation, culture, it takes different strokes for different folks and, from my observations and conversations with those neck-deep in it with me, it's an incredibly personal thing where the journey takes you.

Quite early on in my new life, I'd come up with a little dream for me, in my new role as a single parent.

> LITTLE DREAM: To run a successful business as an openly single mum; it can be done!

I was not going to accept the story that being a single mum was any harder than just being a mum or, if I'm honest, being a human. Today's world is tough and, as naturalist Charles Darwin outlined many moons ago in his theory of evolution designed to explain biological change, it really is survival of the fittest. I hope he wouldn't mind if I add to that criteria: in my opinion, it's also survival of the *most determined*.

Don't ever accept the story you've been handed.
We live in an age where it is the most
determined that survive, not only the fittest ...
the real little-dream chasers.

I've had it said to me on a few occasions that perhaps it's best not to talk about the 'single parent thing' too much within the business context; that by doing so, I am potentially downgrading my professional abilities and shining a light on something that isn't really, well, that attractive to potential clients. One particular businessperson once said to me, 'You need to make a choice, Lisa. Are you a single mum who built a successful PR business? Or are you a successful businesswoman who happens to be single mum?' This question caused me more than a year of internal anguish because, for me, I didn't believe that there needed to be a choice. These descriptions were about two parts of the one me. If I had to dissect it, I'd say I simply see them as different sides of the same coin that can be turned one side or the other, depending on the person and the situation. To make this little dream come true, I purposely weaved the story of how LBPR came to be into the narrative from the get-go.

Recently, a Facebook memory from LBPR popped up from 2015. I remember writing this post *so* vividly. It wasn't usual to talk about your personal life in a business context back then (yes, only five short years ago!). This is what I wrote, word for word:

*DO YOU KNOW WHAT? It's time to get real. I sit here tonight on my laptop in my PJs feeling so blessed to be living in an era where a single mum of two little boys can run a successful and fulfilling PR business. Most of my clients are also mums, and juggling a million balls in the air – and together, whether we know it or not, we are re-writing the rules of engagement when it comes to business.*

*One LBPR client did our weekly TC with me at 8 pm tonight once our children were in bed and the evening chaos was over; another admitted that she goes interstate on works trips whenever she can to have a night alone in a hotel (and I admitted the same thing!). I was quite happy to let another client know I would probably stop breathing if I was forced to play with Lego, do craft and make little cars out of play doh for more than one day a month.*

*I love it that we are all being REAL – about who we are and our lives and how our work fits in. If I am on email at 11pm at night it's not because I am inefficient; it is because I have a LIFE outside of work. Gone are the days where you don't mention your children or your com-mitments outside of work to a client – heaven forbid you actually HAVE a life beyond their brand!*

*Business is getting personal and, in my view, we are all the better for it.*

I look back and love that I had the guts to write that!

I find respect levels rise straight up when clients know where I started: it articulates beautifully that I'm the type of person who captures a little dream, sets some goals, works hard and gets on with it. That's pretty much a rundown of the core attributes clients look for in a consultant.

In the early days, I made sure that, as much as possible, I scheduled calls when Nate was asleep and Luca was at preschool. I'd write proposals and other documents that required zero human interaction once they were in bed. By being honest about the juggle, I find clients know I can serve their needs because they can see I'm super organised, very diligent and incredibly accountable.

There's usually more than one way to do something and, with some foresight and planning, I've shown that it's entirely possible to run and build a great business while you're also building great children as single parent.

And there it was. I'd hatched another little dream for myself.

## LITTLE DREAM RESET: Be present for my children as I build LBPR and them.

It's entirely possible for you to achieve whatever you want to, just by stitching little dreams together in a patchwork quilt that is your vision.
Whether it's like me – to run and build a great business while also building great children as a single parent – or something entirely different, you've got this.

It's always very interesting to me when I see parents who decided to start up their own business so they could spend more time with their children, doing the complete opposite. Please know I write this without judgement; it's just as an observation. I get that raising children is a very hard job and sometimes the paid one is very welcome relief!

My little dream to be there for my boys while running a business is one that is constantly tested. They're young and the situation is ever-changing. One of the biggest shifts for me was Luca starting 'big school'. This means his schooling location and hours are different to Nate's, and there is a much bigger part for parents to play in their child's learning: assemblies and events, homework and projects, to name just some of the parenting requirements that come with the transition to 'big school'.

About three years into running LBPR, my little dream to be a present mum for my real babies (LBPR is always the non-human baby) was getting seriously compromised and I knew I had to work out a way to get it back on track. If the main 'pro' on my list of reasons for creating LBPR wasn't being fulfilled, I knew I might as well shut the doors.

As I didn't want to do that, I needed to reset a little dream, fast. This is important because it may happen to you too; without attention and reminding yourself daily, little dreams can become little more than promises you once made to yourself. I recommend that you diarise weekly checks where you not only measure what you have achieved in terms of actions, but also how you *feel*. Having both these elements in sync is the key to not only achieving a little dream, but also being able to actually enjoy the moment when it comes to fruition!

---

It's perfectly OK to reset your little dreams from time to time; without attention and care they can become little more than promises you once made to yourself.

---

As a business goes through the growth phase, it has the very real potential to consume you. If you've experienced this or are in it now, whether as employer or employee, you'll know as hard and long as you search, there is no off switch. Just like the Magic Pudding, the opportunities are boundless and without some self-regulation, it can become all you think about.

I thought that the best way to solve the competing needs of my human and non-human babies was to get some external help with my boys. My mum and dad helped enormously, but I wanted to ensure they could fulfil their little dreams too, which included being able to travel. I knew other families who employed nannies and au pairs and felt like maybe I should get one too. I narrowed my needs down to school drop-offs and pick-ups, including the night-time bath/dinner routine.

As is my tendency, I explored this option with gusto, found someone who was capable and lovely, and introduced her to my boys. But when it came time to sign contracts and commit, I simply couldn't do it. Once I put myself in a space where I could see and feel what it would be like to drive to LBPR without children to talk to, to leave LBPR at 6 pm and go home to fed and bathed babies, I realised that I was actually going against one of my core reasons for starting the business *plus* giving up incredibly special time with them. I felt like

I was compromising them and, most of all, I was compromising myself and the little dream that was the cornerstone of why I embarked on this crazy business-owner ride in the first place.

I remembered that some of my best conversations with Luca and Nate are had on the way home from school. Luca will tell me about why we need to save the bees and intricate details about the farm he is building with his friends (at last count they're planning on caring for thirty-six goats, two llamas and fifty teacup pigs), while Nate will have a story about his beloved trains and the sandpit chaos they've been in. They ask me all manner of crazy things, usually on the way to school when I am yet to have my caffeine hit.

'Mumma, do you know why horses are only brown and black and white? What about pink?'

'Mom,' (that's Nate, yes he is American apparently) 'if Thomas was a girl, would Percy still be his best friend?'

One of my personal favourites was being asked what my third favourite reptile was on the way home. Yep, not interested in the first and second choice, just the third. (After much careful consideration while I simultaneously navigated the impatient afternoon traffic, I can confirm it's a frillneck lizard).

Every morning and afternoon, for reasons I can't even remember, we have this ritual where I'll turn around from the front seat of the car, we'll stacks on with our hands, and shout at the top of our lungs, 'All for one, and one for ALL!' That's a treasured moment I don't ever, ever want to miss out on.

I also knew, deep down in my heart of hearts, that more time available didn't mean greater efficiency for someone like me, with an innate need to do most things last minute. If I had until 6 pm each night, I probably wouldn't get more done, I'd just procrastinate more.

**Little dreams are promises that you make to yourself that require immediate action. Not tomorrow, not someday, but today.**

There are times when I think the nanny option would have been good, because let's call a spade a spade; bath time and dinner can be totally challenging. I often lose it (as do they), but by the time I get the boys into bed we're all mates again and my parenting cup is full. Most days, I leave the office at 2.30 pm to pick them up and don't sit down to work until 7 pm, if I do any work at all. After nearly five years in business, I know everything will get done one way or another. A lack of available time is a great filter for what's truly urgent and important, and what can wait.

Once I'd decided that the nanny/au pair option wasn't for me, and that my little dream was to be present for my children as I built LBPR, I came up with some alternative options to get through a busy workload:

- Give the urgent task to a member of my team or
- Outsource the urgent task if my core team is too busy
- Renegotiate a deadline with a client
- Take my boys to a play centre where they are amused and I can do what I need to
- Say no.

That last point – saying no – was the hardest of all to implement, but it's now my favourite and is incredibly empowering, once you get into the swing of it! As the meme that periodically does the rounds on social media asks us to consider, 'By saying yes to someone else, make sure you're not saying no to yourself.' Making any decision you need to within that framework makes it so much easier.

Even though the little dream you have may be about you ultimately, always consider how it will positively impact those closest to you. Just like a pebble hitting the surface of the lake, the potential for a positive ripple effect from what you're bringing to fruition is undeniable. In my experience, whatever you want is what those closest to you want for you too, and seeing a little dream of yours intertwine with someone else's is pure magic.

I always remember this beautiful saying: 'The days are long, but the years are short.' It won't be long before my boys won't need their mumma to drop and pick them up from school, or they'll think our 'all for one' ritual is for dorks. So for now, I'll soak up as much as I can get – including the tricky questions about reptiles.

Take some time now to revisit the little dreams you wrote down at the start of this book and make a note of the people who will be impacted or a part of what you're seeking. Even though my children were little babies when I started my business, I know that me considering them and being physically and emotionally there for them is what they wanted (and needed) too.

## Another little dream had come true.

---

# Little Dreams Never Run Out Of Steam

Do you know what I love most about little dreams? They're not one-hit wonders, they never run out and they keep giving to you, long after you've achieved their first iteration. Let me tell you a quick story to show you what I mean.

Do you remember the first little dream of mine in this book? I set up LBPR so I could be a present single mum to my two little boys. (LITTLE DREAM: To have my own business so I can always be there for my boys.)

At the start of a very busy week, my son Nate had an accident requiring surgery in Sydney. This meant time off work and complete focus on him. Did I have to call my boss? No. Did I need permission? No. Did I have the full support of my LBPR team to do what I had to, without concern that the wheels of the business would fall off? Yes, without question.

Interestingly, the timing of this stressful situation with Nate coincided with the Public Relations Institute of Australia Awards and I was all set to go. LBPR was a finalist in two categories: Best Small PR Consultancy and Best Small Budget PR Campaign, the latter for our work with Girl Guides Australia to promote the Diamond Anniversary of their much-loved annual Biscuit Drive.

Excitingly, we won both categories – such a thrill for the team and me! But I wasn't there to receive the awards, nor celebrate. I was in a children's hospital with my son, making sure he was calm and supported by me, his mum. Pretty dresses and champagne can wait; little boys who need their mums can't.

If ever there was a tangible example of a little dream continuing to deliver, this was it. I created LBPR to be a present mum, and here I was, being just that! I was right where I was meant to be.

My little dream came true … again. And guess what? All the best ones do; they love coming back to you again and again.

# 07

# The home

# that Lisa built

# built

Home is where the heart is. I didn't really understand the depth of that statement until I was living in a house that didn't have one. Once I was a single mum and the boys' dad had left, I used to sit in our Kiama house on the South Coast of New South Wales in Australia, where I'd hoped for so many memories that were never going to come to life, and it felt so cold and empty. There was no heart left and I couldn't see myself staying there. Although I had the option to take on the mortgage by myself, the truth was it wasn't a *viable* option. No bank was going to agree to hand over the title deeds and that level of financial responsibility to a single mum without a steady job and regular income.

I was so mad at myself for being in this position and vowed to myself that I'd never let this happen again. I'd work my bottom off to get a home for us, and it would be ours forever. Somewhere to always hang our hats, no matter where life took the three of us.

In Kiama, there is a beautiful yet eerie place called Storm Bay. During this time of limbo, when I knew we couldn't stay in Kiama but I didn't know what to do next, I'd bundle the boys up in the pram and we'd sit there together. The constant crashing of the waves against the dark rocks was also meditative and I think that's why I gravitated to that spot at least a few times a week. It was there that I decided I'd like LBPR to grow to the point where I could buy a house for my little family.

Now, that was definitely in big dream territory at that point and I knew it, so I didn't dwell on it too much. Rather, that dream was placed in the back of my mind and I only thought about it consciously when I went to Storm Bay. Over a period of four months, I simply created a few little dreams in my head to get to that bigger dream, giving myself four years to achieve my ultimate goal.

---

Simply create a few little dreams in your head to get to that bigger dream and agree on a timeframe with yourself to achieve your ultimate goal.

---

It was also at Storm Bay that I faced reality. I realised I'd have to rent somewhere in the short term and I decided to move to Wollongong, back to where I grew up. LBPR had a steady enough income to be able to get a landlord, a beautiful lady I knew through another friend, to agree to take me on, and the boys and I quickly settled into our temporary home in an inner-city apartment. After the eerie stillness of Kiama, the buzz of the city was just what the doctor ordered. I felt alive; part of the human race again.

> What can start out as thoughts sitting on the virtual banks of a river in your mind, can turn into the most wonderful reality when you stick at it, commit to your vision, and never, ever give up.

## A PICTURE TELLS A THOUSAND WORDS

As I embarked on the LBPR journey, I met a talented artist called Kathy Karas. Based in Kiama, Kathy paints beautiful artwork that captures the heart and soul of the natural landscape. One day, as I was looking at her latest pieces on Facebook, there it was – Storm Bay. Kathy had painted it from the viewpoint where the audience was looking straight at the very spot where I used to sit with the boys and plan my little dreams to ultimately secure a home for us.

I knew I had to have that painting, and so I saved my pennies and bought it. I wanted it to sit opposite my bed in my yet-to-be-purchased house. I wanted to wake up each morning and, before the craziness of the day started, see that past version of me sitting there in the painting, sad but hopeful. I wanted to be able to say to her, 'See Lis? You did it! *You did it*. Here I am in your home. I'm so pleased you kept dreaming little dreams to make this happen. Thank you.'

This daily visual reminder is so important because it energises me in ways that are supernatural. It reminds me to keep on keeping on with my little dreams. What starts as thoughts sitting on the banks of an eerie bay in a small town can turn into the most wonderful reality when you stick at it and never, ever give up.

Do you have a memento or item that can serve as a reminder of how far you've come? When you commit to a little dream, find something that will take you back to the start. It's such a simple yet powerful way to help you see how far you've come.

---

## LITTLE DREAM: Get a home loan as a single mum running her own business

---

When I told my family and close friends about my (slightly bigger) little dream to buy a house they got behind me 100 per cent. I'm sure you can remember a time when you proclaimed something that was a little unrealistic at the time, but your cheer squad threw up their virtual pom poms regardless because they believed in your ability to achieve what you said you would.

However, when you announce the same little dream to members of your extended advisory team who don't have emotional attachment to you – like bank mortgage lenders, mortgage brokers and accountants – it gets very interesting.

I vividly remember the first conversation with my accountant about me buying a house at some point. Getting a home loan was little dream number one and it came to me when I was less than a year into my business-owning journey. My accountant knew a single mum owning a start-up was pretty much the worst combination of factors to present to a bank manager or mortgage broker. Of course, I knew it too, but I also knew that stability for my children in terms of a place to call home and financial security for us all were key drivers for me. They were non-negotiables. It wasn't an impossible dream; it was really a little dream that just needed an injection of unrelenting dedication, constant action and unwavering self-belief.

## No dream is ever impossible: they're really a little dream in need of an injection of unrelenting dedication, gumption and unwavering self-belief.

I told him I wanted to do it because my heart told me to, that I *would* do it, and we needed to structure things to ensure it happened, pending my ability to build the business to a sustainable and financially profitable model. To his credit, he hopped on the bandwagon and helped me.

One of the primary motivators – actually the number-one motivator for getting my business to a financially attractive point – was to be able to secure a mortgage so I could buy a house. Security was understandably on top of my values list at this point in time; I was tired of moving (having done so every year since I was eighteen years old) and my boys needed a place to call home.

I knew leaving the house in Kiama wasn't a great decision financially, especially when the property market was booming, but my mental health was so important to get right. I wasn't going to feel better, and therefore grow a business and be a good mum in surroundings that reminded me of sad times.

So, what did I do? What I always do!

I started dreaming little. This meant simply putting out feelers with a lending manager at my local bank branch. I had a steady roster of clients that paid me promptly, my overheads were low as I was operating out of a bedroom in the rented apartment we'd moved to after Kiama while I figured out what next, and I had one part-time staff member. Of course, I knew what I looked like through his lens – a single mum and self-employed. It wasn't exactly gold-star material in the criteria for assessing mortgage feasibility.

I was banking (pun intended) on him also being able to *see* me: ambitious, hard-working and someone who had built a business quickly to this point, against a pretty dismal backdrop. A good long-term bet.

'I know how you see me,' I said to him, as I wanted to call it early. 'But I know I am a better bet than at least 50 per cent of the people you've given mortgages to. This is just the beginning; if I can get a mortgage for one house I'll be back for more as the business grows. I have the deposit ready. Oh, and I've been paying more in rent for about twelve months and never missed a payment.'

This man of a similar age to me held all the virtual cards across his sterile desk. He tapped his branded pen on the edge of his calculator. 'Lisa,' he said, 'I don't doubt you have ambition and drive. But these are not qualities our mortgage lenders assess against. I suggest you adjust your goals; keep renting. A roof over your head is a big achievement for a single mum.'

Wow. Wow. Wow.

I bet you can imagine my face and the internal rage I felt inside at this outcome. If he'd offered to see me again in six months, perhaps given me some numbers to work towards, well that would have been great. But no. He was done with me, and with that comment, I was done with him. When faced with obstacles and opinions, you can choose to turn back and believe what others say. That's the easy option for sure. But me? I wasn't having a bar of his view.

---

When faced with obstacles and opinions, you can choose to turn back and believe what others say. That's the easy option for sure. But is it the option that will bring your little dream to life?

---

I politely thanked him for his time, left his office, and sat in a nearby cafe hatching a plan B.

At this time, I was a part of a local business networking group and there was a mortgage broker who attended. I figured he'd be willing to help me and at the very least map out a plan; he knew my story and he understood how driven I was … well, at least I thought he did.

I sent him an email about wanting to buy a house and we agreed to meet after our next fortnightly meeting. After telling him excitedly about my plans and how I was truly ready to do whatever I had to in order to get a mortgage over the line, I was smacked down faster than you can say bow-bow, *The Price is Right*-style. 'Lisa, in all honesty, no bank is going to back you. You're a single mum and you have a small business. I can't help you.'

It was quick, like ripping off a bandaid, and I was shocked. This hurt me far more than the first knockback, as I had assumed a more personal connection meant at the very least this person would want to step up to the challenge and try. I also figured a mortgage broker could speak to a number of banks, so a knockback with one didn't mean a no across the board.

Once again, I was disappointed and deflated, but in true optimist style, I picked myself up fairly soon after. I decided to stop forcing it and simply sit tight, continue working hard and trust the timing of the universe to deliver what I was feverishly wishing for. Patience is a virtue and, while it's not my natural default position, I knew it was needed for the little dreams I had linked to the house. This is really important to remember: even little dreams take time and letting them take shape rather than forcing it reaps significant dividends in the end – because they come true!

> Remember this: even little dreams take time and letting them take shape rather than forcing it reaps significant dividends in the end – because they come true!

The universe did deliver, in two seemingly unlinked but completely intertwined ways.

The first was a wonderful man (and now friend), Terry, whom I met through an amazing organisation called Illawarra Women in Business. Terry happened to be a mortgage lender. He knew my story and became instrumental to me securing my home loan about six months later. He clearly saw my potential and that of my business.

By the time our paths crossed, I had some more impressive numbers under my belt that clearly demonstrated consistency and a path of solid growth, plus a spreadsheet that could predict fairly accurately what the twelve months ahead looked like. I had purchase orders from clients, which you'll remember I noted early on as important because they are a pretty good indicator the work will be paid for! He was on my team and willing to go into bat for me, and I can never thank him enough.

## A little dream had come true.

In tandem, my business secured a new client that specialised in building homes. They came to me as they'd experienced some unfair media coverage based on a previous franchise owner who didn't do the right thing; houses were left half built and what was built was shoddy, to say the very least. My new client decided to fix these homes for free, as they simply couldn't sleep at night with a roof over their heads knowing there were people linked to their business who didn't have a home at all. Part of my remit was to call these people with now completed homes and write up their stories, to offer to the media.

As I called these people, a little seed was planted and slowly watered. I started to think about building a home, rather than buying one. Of course, I'd heard the horror stories about slack tradies, blown-out budgets and slipping timelines. But this client's values and ethics, coupled with the way these now-happy homeowners spoke about them, made up my mind.

I wasn't going to buy a home: I was going to build one.

## LITTLE DREAM: Build a new home; design it myself from top to bottom!

Once that decision was made, and my mortgage was approved, it was all systems go. I moved out of the apartment into my parents' house to save money. Moving home at forty with two children isn't usual but we had such a special time and I am eternally grateful to my mum and dad for having us.

I thoroughly enjoyed every single moment of the house-building process, especially designing the layout to suit my little family (there is no design like ours). The day I got to choose the interior finishes, from paint to taps to door handles and flooring was just like that scene in *Pretty Woman* where Richard Gere takes Julia Roberts to Rodeo Drive and she can pick whatever she wants. I felt just like she must have (minus the sex worker part, obviously).

Three years after that first conversation with the first bank manager who told me I should stick to renting, I moved into my beautiful new home nestled at the foot of a truly awe-inspiring mountain range, one year ahead of the already-ambitious timeline I'd set myself sitting at Storm Bay in Kiama. My boys watched with me as the slab went down, the frame went up and the roof went on. To see their excited little faces at knowing this was their home too – and yes, they had their own rooms and space enough in the backyard for a dog one day – filled my heart to the point of bursting. I actually gave myself permission to be proud of me the day I got the keys and we officially moved in.

## A little (maybe slightly bigger!) dream had come true.

We've now been in our home for a few years and it has made a huge difference to my happiness and that of my boys. We have made so many amazing memories already and I often sit in the back room, where the ceiling is pitched high enough for me to see the mountain range, and marvel at the fact I did it.

My series of little dreams coming true led to a pretty massive one coming true. I built my own home as a single mum running her own business.

When I think about life in my mind's eye it's always a necklace, and the little dreams are beads. Round and round the beads go, held tightly together by a chain or string; a never-ending stream of moments. Nestled side by side, the beads or little dreams create your reality. Inevitably little dreams come true and suddenly your necklace, the big dream, is complete. This is the circle of life.

## ALL IT TAKES IS A LITTLE GUMPTION: STEPS TO TAKE NOW

I do hope after reading about my personal experiences in Part 2 you can see the enormous benefits being who you are at the core, in work and play, and that you're inspired to give it a go!

What are *your* little dreams when it comes to being who you really are? How can you use that to propel you forward? Write your little dream down here (remember, you may have captured this at the start of the book too).

Be as descriptive as you can and use the SMART framework – Specific, Measurable, Achievable, Realistic and Timebound – to make it tangible.

To help you, here's what mine looked like at the start of the LBPR journey:

*My dream a little dream is to run a successful business as an openly single mum; it can be done! To achieve this, I'll put my personal story and the reason I set up the business in all communications from February 2014.*

Refer back to the DNA of a little dream at the start of this book if you need some clarity.

### *MY LITTLE DREAM IS ...*

_____

_____

_____

_____

_____

**THIS LITTLE DREAM IS IMPORTANT TO ME BECAUSE ...**

_____

_____

_____

_____

**I NEED THESE PEOPLE OR RESOURCES TO HELP ME REALISE THIS LITTLE DREAM ...**

_____

_____

_____

_____

Now you have this little dream captured, write down at least four steps you can take right now to make it come true. To help you, here's my task list linked to my little dreams around being true to myself:

- Write the core copy that will explain how LBPR was born and my role as a single parent in this narrative
- Share this copy with two clients I trust to ensure it resonates; make tweaks as needed
- Include approved copy on LBPR website and in credentials, social media posts and award entries
- Measure value of this story in business success - attracting new clients and retaining current clients, securing quality employees and award recognition.

**MY LITTLE DREAM TASK LIST IS...**

1. _____

2. _____

3. _____

4. _____

5. _____

All you need to make a little dream come true is a clear idea of what it is and some clear actions. Seems simple, doesn't it? That's because it is!

You can repeat this exercise for as many little dreams as you like. There is no limit – however, I'd recommend keeping it to a maximum of six. Otherwise you run the risk of veering into big dream territory and that's where overwhelm and inertia are waiting to greet you.

**Dream small and keep moving.**

**That's all you need to do to make it happen.**

# THOUGHT SPARK: History never repeats ...
## or does it?

After much reflection, I absolutely believe being a single parent was always going to be my path and I am so grateful for the opportunities it has given me. I know, it's weird to say that, but being a single parent and throwing running a business into the mix has forced me to get amazingly good at managing myself. It has done so in terms of both the functional and emotional requirements of being a human, and in a way people who aren't single parents can never fully comprehend or understand. I have grown (up?) as a person because of this reality and I don't believe I'd have the same grit, tenacity and resilience without it.

In a very cool discovery, I only found out quite recently that my great-grandmother on my mum's side of the family, Myrtle, was a single parent too. While the circumstances were different – my grandfather became very sick and died – our lives have some distinct similarities. Myrtle was born in 1894 and had three very young girls to raise in the early-1900s. She worked hard at sewing and other 'female' jobs to ensure she could care for her girls. No doubt she was smart but in those days education wasn't a priority for women and being a single mum was often a ticket to social exclusion.

Fast forward to 2018 and her great-granddaughter – that's me – is also an unexpectedly single mum, with two very young boys to raise. But, unlike her, I am educated. Unlike her, I had the choice to start my own business doing something I love. Unlike her, my single mum status has led to me being embraced and included in worlds I wouldn't have ever been a part of, including entrepreneurship.

Unlike her, I have grown up being told I can do and be anything I want to. I am so grateful today's world allows me to be all I want to and that the fact I'm a single parent, and a woman, is inconsequential. I am so grateful I am alive today and experiencing being a single parent. I hope my great-nanna is proud of me. I am absolutely certain she planted all of the little dreams I've had around evolving the narrative that still lingers around single parents and who are are/are not in today's world, Knowing I'm doing this for her too gives me the courage and drive to be the example of a better way; to show that it can be a blessing, not a burden.

*Is there something in your family that happened in a past generation that you're experiencing now? How it is different for you? Is it better – or are there more challenges? How can you take this recurring situation and shape a little dream around it, creating a new reality for you and your future family members? Capture it below!*

**MY LITTLE DREAM TO ADDRESS A RECURRING SITUATION IN MY FAMILY IS ...**

_____

_____

_____

_____

**THIS LITTLE DREAM IS IMPORTANT TO ME BECAUSE ...**

_____

_____

_____

_____

**I NEED THESE PEOPLE OR RESOURCES TO HELP ME REALISE THIS LITTLE DREAM ...**

_____

_____

_____

_____

_____

_____

_____

# PART 3

## Dreaming of

## BEING INSPIRED

# You can achieve more than you think you can

# 08

# Recognition IS NOT a dirty word

Let me ask you this - and please answer inside your own head honestly. How much weight do you place on the opinion of others? Are you more likely to say to yourself, 'I'll do what I want, regardless of what people say,' or is your life more likely to follow a mind that says, 'I'm not sure people will expect that of me, so I won't do it ... better to stay between the lines of life, than colour outside'?

have almost always been the latter: a conformer, rather than a creator of my life. I thank my lucky stars that I woke up to myself when my world collapsed around me and realised this life, in this body, with this brain, is not a dress rehearsal. We don't get to go back and try again, give it another shot, or say yes when we said no.

Recently, I made a non-negotiable commitment to myself that, until I close my eyes for the last time, I'm going to care very little about what others think unless it's adding genuine value to my life and my vision. Instead, I'm going to pay far more attention to what *I* think. I'm going to do all the things I want to in my head and heart without delay because I don't want to get to the end and say things to myself like: 'Oh shit, I wanted to write a book and now it's too damn late.' (Thankfully, as you can see, I won't be saying *that* to myself!)

Long gone are the days where I second guess myself, think I'm not good enough or believe that my ideas or plans for a future that's a bit different to what I had planned, or others thought for me, are just 'flights of fancy'. Now I instead think of what I'm doing as life purpose-fuelled, genuine contributions in which others may find some value. I finally feel that I am worthy regardless of the views and opinions of others.

Of course, I have only reached this point in my heart and head because I *have* cared what people think for a number of years, frequently seeking external validation to verify my internal worth-o-meter via recognition of some sort. I've found the journey of recognition, whether it's professional or personal, to be an interesting one. It can consume you or it can propel you forward. In fact, it relies almost entirely on *future you* pulling you forward.

The journey of recognition is all about doing something that's a bit scary where the outcome is unpredictable. You almost always will start putting yourself forward to acquire validation that you're doing well against your peers or those you admire. Somewhere along the line the journey starts to lead to new opportunities because you're willing to step outside of your comfort zone, put your head above the parapet and have a go. Yes: your future self steps in and you decide to step up and meet life's opportunities head on. I'm getting goosebumps writing this to you, as I know this is where there are *so* many little dreams you'll be hard pressed not to start tripping over them!

As my experience will now show you, once you put yourself out there a few times, having a go at little dreams, something amazing happens: the recognition pendulum starts to swing and you find some amazing opportunities coming your way purely because you were willing to put yourself out there first. This is the magic moment where you start to experience the unexpected little dreams ... the ones that you weren't seeking, but that found you.

---

It is a magic moment when you start to experience unexpected little dreams ... the ones that you weren't seeking, but that found you, simply because you made yourself known. Be careful, as you might start to have so many little dreams that you're tripping over them. Oh, what a wonderful place to find yourself!

---

One of the best added benefits that recognition can give you is opportunity. Recognition can be internal or external and validating yourself is extremely important. I am getting much better at being able to do this as I get older but I won't lie: for me, being recognised as doing good work by others and being seen as human being contributing in a positive way to personal and professional networks, boosts my self-confidence and most importantly encourages me to expand my contribution to the world.

Here's some social proof of that thought process: the book you have in your hands right now wouldn't exist without the 'shot in the arm' I've received from others whose opinion I value telling me to keep going. Putting LBPR and myself out there for judgement and benchmarking has also been the breeding ground of some of my deepest friendships, strongest connections and greatest learnings.

For me, recognition definitely goes *way* deeper than a trophy on the shelf or a certificate on the wall. It's not only a great chance to reflect on how far I've come, but also to see how I'm tracking against others in the same professional field, or at a similar stage of their professional journey.

---

Recognition definitely goes way deeper than a trophy on the shelf or a certificate on the wall.
Little dreams that centre on you putting yourself out there can deliver deep friendships, strong connections and great learnings.

---

I'm sure I'm not alone in feeling a sense of encouragement and achievement when someone, or a group of people, deems me worthy of recognition. You know that feeling too, right? The fact is human beings are programmed to seek recognition from the moment we are born, from learning human basics like crawling, walking and talking to entering the school gates and then the workforce. The need for some sort of acknowledgement for a job well done starts young and is fostered throughout life.

What I've noticed during my lifetime is that a little or big pat on the back - whether it's from someone older, more experienced or just a little bit ahead of you on this journey called life - can have a hugely positive impact regardless of your age or life stage. It can foster new connections, improve self-worth, create new opportunities and take you on an adventure of which you didn't even dare dream. I see it with my boys now: a certificate from school, a trophy at the end of the soccer season; all these little achievements help remind us we are a part of something special and that we are important.

Alan Alda of *M*A*S*H* fame said, 'Awards can give you a tremendous amount of encouragement to keep getting better, no matter how young or old you are.' I think he's right. Of course, I know awards and recognition can get a bad rap; they're often seen as the domain of the ego-driven attention seeker. However, I firmly believe throwing your hat in the ring shows tremendous bravery and a desire to keep getting better. Whether that's on a personal or professional level; whether it's an individual pat on the back or group recognition; whether it's internal or external, you always feel part of something special and driven to do and be more.

As a PR professional, I know the value of others recognising what I am doing. Advertising is what you say about yourself, but PR is what others say about you and, therefore, arguably of more value.

Because I started LBPR and my business journey at the exact same time I was rebuilding myself as a person, I'll admit I was seeking external recognition that I was doing well more than most people. My family and close friends told me they were proud of me, and that was, and still is, very special and important. But when somebody who doesn't know you thinks what you're up to is noteworthy, well, that has the power to completely transform the lens through which you view yourself and your whole life.

Entering LBPR into awards was a no brainer. This doesn't mean I wasn't scared; I was petrified. When you put yourself out there, things don't always go the way you want them to and I knew I needed to have enough internal strength and belief to deal with not being the award winner. After much thought, this little dream started to take shape:

what was the worst that could happen if I didn't win? Nothing! It just meant it wasn't my time, I'd learn and would go back the next year.

I knew pitting me and my business against others on the same path was the best way to see how I was doing. I'd never run a business before and I had no idea if what I was doing was equal to, or ahead of, others walking alongside me. I was eager to learn and saw entering awards as a way to meet other business owners I may never have found, to hear their stories and be inspired to continue my own.

It's also a milestone that you can celebrate with your team if you have one. There's no 'I' in team and working together to achieve an award you're all proud of can create a sense of team cohesion like no other. American writer Dale Carnegie was onto something when he said, 'People work for money but go the extra mile for recognition, praise and rewards.'

---

## LITTLE DREAM: LBPR to be recognised with an award from my local business community.

---

My first little dream was to see if my local business community thought LBPR was doing well. There were two opportunities – Illawarra Women in Business and the Illawarra Business Chamber – so I wrote entries for both, targeting the Best New Business categories. Writing good award entries takes time and I would spend my child-free weekends tapping away alone in LBPR's little first office space, ensuring I did LBPR justice with my responses. I also, just for fun, submitted an entry for the Businesswoman of the Year category in the Illawarra Women in Business awards. Why not? I had zero expectations for that one; I just wanted to have a go and have something for my future self to pick up as another little dream to pursue at some point.

As I put down my thoughts in writing, I felt enormous pride at what had been achieved by LBPR and me personally in just twelve months, against a challenging backdrop: amazing clients from in and outside of our geographical area, attracting a talented team which meant creation of local employment opportunities, a need for a professional office space sooner than expected due to phenomenal growth, and the delivery of workshops about PR specifically for small business, reaching ninety local owners at three events. I included client testimonials, financials, letters of support from my team and examples of campaigns on which we'd worked. If you're going to nominate for an award, then you really need to spend the time pulling together an award-winning entry!

Without an award for which to strive and an entry to write, I can tell you now I wouldn't have taken the time to reflect with my team and myself on the journey to date, and that's one hell of a missed opportunity. It's not until you stop to take not of what's happened that you realise all the little dreams that have come true, right under your feet! Awards also provided a lovely avenue through which clients could tell us what they thought. The entire LBPR team felt enormous pride when we read what they thought of LBPR: 'strategic partner,' 'extended member of the team' and 'we can't imagine not working with LBPR' were some of the beautiful comments our clients wrote to support our award entries.

Thrillingly, we reached the interview stage for all three entries and this was the best part for me. Sure, I was really nervous, but I also knew that I could bring the words on paper to life in person. I was being interviewed and probed about a topic I knew everything about; there could be no trick questions. Verbalising what LBPR stood for, where it came from (including my personal story), and where it was going gave me so much joy. Each judge listened intently, and they were so complimentary about the story I had to share. A few tears were shed as my story touched their own. At this stage of the process, I truly felt like I'd won already. It was such a positive experience.

'I am definitely not willing to live a
"should have, could have" life anymore, and,
despite my extreme nervousness and fear at
pushing forward into uncharted territory,
I almost always go for it because regret is a
far heavier burden. In these moments,
I always pretend I'm my future self.
What will future Lisa say if I do it/don't do it?
I firmly believe the opinion of your future
self is such a great way to give yourself a
virtual kick up the backside.
What keeps me pushing forward is this pertinent
question: imagine missing an opportunity –
a little dream – that could have changed your life?'

The next step was to attend the actual award events. To sit and wait for your name to be called out - or not called out - is never a fun thing for me, or anyone for that matter. But I wasn't known at this point so I was the underdog in every sense. If I didn't do well, it really didn't matter. I'd talked myself out of the idea of LBPR winning and decided in advance to find the person who did win, so I could learn from them afterwards.

I'm proud to say that LBPR did win these two local business awards and I was also very shocked (and pleasantly surprised) to be awarded Highly Commended for Illawarra Businesswoman of the Year. After being so unsure as to whether starting a business was a good idea, after all of the sleepless nights and hard work that nobody saw but me, this recognition was like a shot of adrenaline in the arm. I was on the right track and I was doing well. We attracted some new clients to LBPR too as our profile increased; that was a wonderful benefit and

I'm proud to say these businesses remain our valued clients to this day.

Each judge said to me afterwards, without fail, 'Keep going, Lisa.' And so I did (and continue to; I'm a bit like the human version of a runaway train when it comes to making little dreams come true!). I've never had a judging panel that has been anything other than supportive of what I'm saying either. Their interest is genuine and I'm still in touch with many people who've met me through this avenue; they remain interested in where I'm at and what I'm doing now.

You'll also meet and connect with so many new people and get a shot of inspiration that spurs you on to your next goal. I looked at which businesses and people had been awarded in the categories I felt were appropriate for LBPR and me for the next year. I researched what they'd done and even met up with two of them to understand their business journey in more detail. What struck me with each and every person was their generosity - they shared intimate details of their business with me and, on one occasion, I was emailed their actual award entries! I've now had the privilege of being able to do this for other people entering awards with which I've had experience.

I took what I could from this fact-finding mission that could be applied to my business and implemented it. The overarching theme of all businesses I interacted with in this way was continuing to grow in a managed way, do good work, be true to their professional values (yes, all the winners had these, which is very telling!), and retain staff through recognition and excellent working conditions. Who knew putting LBPR and myself forward for awards could deliver these added benefits?

The following year, LBPR was recognised as Best Small Business by Illawarra Women in Business and I was personally awarded Illawarra Businesswoman of the Year and Innovative Businesswoman of the Year. The latter award was for LBPR's Catalyst, Australia's first student consultancy (you'll recall LBPR's Catalyst from Part 2 of this book).

## Another little dream had come true.

Unsurprisingly, that day was one of the best days of my entire life. It is a constant and fond reminder that dreaming little is all it takes to achieve big stuff.

## Dreaming little is all it takes for you to achieve the big stuff.

Me being me – ambitious, driven and up for a challenge – I decided to map out some more little dreams centred on putting LBPR forward for PR industry recognition. This was really important to me personally too; with a twenty-plus-year PR career under my belt, having my peers hear my story and possibly award LBPR, was an intoxicating thought. You probably have awards for your industry or profession that recognise excellence; they are worth exploring if you haven't already.

## LITTLE DREAM: LBPR to be recognised as best in class by the PR industry.

I approached this award as I did the local ones – I poured my heart onto the page. Differentiating yourself from others is key so I led with my personal story – a single mum setting up a business at the worst possible time – and weaved in tales of client success, financial achievement, training small business on PR's importance and creating employment opportunities for our industry.

Excitingly, LBPR was named a NSW finalist in the NSW Micro Consultancy of the Year category. The awards event was in Sydney. I took my best friend Roger with me and, as always, my default position was to have little or no expectation LBPR could win.

Finally, just before LBPR's category was to be announced, Rog was standing near the presentation and he could already see the next slide in preview mode: 'Burlo! You bloody did it! Get up there, *get up there!*' Wow-wee – we did it! I was speechless; I couldn't believe it. This was the icing on the cake for me in the early days of LBPR.

## A little dream had come true.

LBPR was Highly Commended at the national level, which was just as it should be at that stage of the business's existence and still an amazing outcome.

It also became really important to also put forward the PR campaigns on which we were working. Our clients trust us with their vision and message, and I knew some of the work we were doing was incredibly special. In partnership with our clients, we have been awarded every year by PRIA nationally for our PR campaigns

## Another little dream had come true.

# 09

# OPPORTUNITY

# KNOCKS-

# LOUDLY!

While in most cases recognition is a planned little dream, opportunity is most definitely an unexpected little dream. I mentioned previously that recognition leads to opportunity. How do I know? Because it's happened to me more times than I can recount in a way that will keep you engaged with this book! So, let me tell you about just two amazing opportunities that came my way, which I would never have been given had I not put myself out there in my local business community and the PR industry.

---

*While recognition is a little dream you plan for in most cases, opportunity is most definitely an unexpected little dream that wanders up quite unexpectedly, offering you something very special – if you're brave enough to go for it.*

---

The first came from my high school, Keira High. Unbeknownst to me, they recognise a former student each year that the teachers and prefects believe demonstrates the school motto, 'Excelsior'. A Latin word, it's often translated as 'ever upward' or 'still higher'. The Deputy Principal asked me to speak to a group of girls as part of International Women's Day after reading about me in the local newspaper.

I did that (what an experience, walking back into your former high school as a woman and talking to your fifteen-year-old self!), and it went well, so we stayed in touch and the school followed what I was up to. Unbeknownst to me, the teachers and prefects had decided that, based on what they'd seen, I was worthy of the Excelsior award in 2017. No entry was written and there was no judging panel to talk to. I was just being myself and doing my best work. How awesome is that?!

When I took the Principal's call about this award, I genuinely thought he was after some suggestions from me as to who may be suitable. He explained what the award was, why it was special and the traits of the person who usually received the award. I listened intently, racking my brains as to whom I knew from school that could be suitable.

'Lisa, we'd be so honoured if you'd accept the Excelsior award this year.'

Me? I was shocked and touched and proud all at once! In that moment, on that call, I felt like recognition from my high school was the ultimate accolade. Life was coming full circle. It showed me that recognition comes in many forms and presents wonderful chances to connect to people with whom you wouldn't normally have the chance.

As part of the presentation of this award, I was asked to give a short speech to the Year 11 and 12 students in the audience and their parents. Now, that is a gift not handed to many. I took this request seriously and spoke about how the term 'entrepreneur' didn't exist for me when I was at school, and that now it did, the sky was the limit for us all to make a difference however we can; to be the change we want to see in the world. I received emails after that from students, which filled my heart with pure joy. If I helped just one of them be brave, taking the steps to go after what they want, then I am one very happy human. What a reward that was!

---

## An *unexpected* little dream had come true.

---

If you need more convincing that recognition can lead to opportunity, then strap yourself in for another real-life example.

I don't know if you've heard of Inspiring Rare Birds but, assuming not, let me explain. Founded by Australian entrepreneur Jo Burston, this global initiative equips, encourages and enables female entrepreneurs to achieve goals, with an emphasis on learning tools and resources, while connecting them with leading female entrepreneurs in their community. Unofficially, the Rare Birds goal is to change the misconception held by young girls that a criterion for being an entrepreneur is being male. Specifically, the mission is to create change and opportunity for women, building a community of one million women entrepreneurs globally by 2020.

Truth be told, I'd never heard of it until it fell into my lap. The General Manager of Wollongong's destination business (known publicly as Wollongong Press Play) Mark Sleigh, knew of me because I'd put myself out there and created a profile through the local business awards (see how recognition can have *so* many additional benefits?). Mark knew Jo and could see that our region didn't yet have an ambassador. Quick as a flash, he put a call in to Jo recommending me for the role.

And that was how it happened. The ambassador's primary goal is to foster a passion in local women for their own businesses, helping them handle the real-life challenges that go with it by providing practical advice and tools to do so.

I remember exactly where I was when Jo called: in the carpark of the BP petrol station at Sydney Airport! After our telephone conversation, I knew this was something I wanted to be an active part of. So I said yes, despite not really identifying as an entrepreneur yet. We had a wonderful launch event and we have gone on to host a number of practical workshops for local businesswomen on important topics, such as mentoring and building a business strategy. I've found this whole experience to be so positive and love the connection and inspiration the Rare Birds community gives me.

Perhaps the biggest gift Jo and the Rare Birds movement has given me is the belief I am more than a business owner: I am an entrepreneur and that changes the game. It means that I am undefined in many ways and I am free (like a bird, see what I did there?) to explore ideas and come up with solutions for challenges in business, especially for women.

## Another little *unexpected* dream had come true.

Sometimes, little dreams happen without you even needing to dream them yourself. This is the perfect example of how being brave enough to put yourself out there for recognition, combined with being open to new opportunities and going for it, can create some of the most powerful experiences of your life. Remember, this exciting opportunity happened just three short years after I set up my business – purely because I kept dreaming little.

> Sometimes, little dreams happen without you even needing to dream them yourself. Being brave enough to put yourself out there for recognition, combined with being open to new opportunities and a little gumption, can create some of the most powerful experiences of your life.

# 10

# Moving into

# uncharted
# territory

Over the last few years, I've started to identify more and more as an entrepreneur. Specifically, I increasingly see myself as a single mum entrepreneur. This is really exciting: we are fed so many stereotypes about entrepreneurs today (think men working in tech with laptops) that I felt this was a space I could step into and help champion.

Fortunately for me, an organisation already existed that would enable me to shift and pivot into this new identity, if I wanted. Talented sisters, Peace Mitchell and Katy Garner, started the AusMumpreneur Network almost ten years ago and, since then, it has become a powerful and inspiring network for mums who are creating and building businesses. As Australia's number one community for mumpreneurs, it attracts mums who are creating freedom, flexibility, family time, success and the money for themselves and their families. Women just like me.

## LITTLE DREAM: For me to be recognised as an entrepreneur in my own right

Nearly five years after my business journey started, I decided that the time was right to have a go at entering their annual AusMumpreneur Awards. I'd watched from the sidelines for long enough. It was time to step onto the field and see if I had what it took to play, and play well, in a new game.

I looked at the categories and one stood out to me: Rising Star AusMumpreneur of the Year. This award recognises exceptional first-time business owners who have been in business for two to five years. I had no valid reason not to have a go, so I pulled together my written entry and sent it off. Because this one was about me, writing the entry was hugely cathartic. I was forced to go back to day one of my personal and business journey, and document all that had happened. I cried, I smiled but, most of all, I felt proud. The positive experience had already begun!

About a month later, I received an email to let me know I was a national finalist; there were fourteen of us chosen from thousands of entries around Australia. I don't know why, but my initial reaction was 'It's not a big deal.' I didn't say anything to anyone for two weeks. Part of my hesitation was definitely because a condition of being eligible was to attend the AusMumpreneur conference in Melbourne in a few weeks so I could face a judging panel. That sounded a bit scary and logistically it required some major planning to ensure care for my boys.

Recognising the deadline was looming to confirm my attendance, I told a few people about it. Their collective response made me see that this *was* in fact a big deal and that to have come this far in a national award for entrepreneurs was something of which to be immensely proud. So, I put it on my personal and LBPR's social media, told my local newspaper, asked my mum and dad to have my boys. The news was out and the logistics arranged. I was going to Melbourne.

You'll remember me saying that awards deliver well beyond the trophy, and this is the best example I personally have of that being the case. I was beyond nervous attending this conference, as I knew nobody. Not a soul. I turned up on day one, joined the queue to get in and guess what? Everyone else felt the same way! I made four new friends within two minutes and I lost count of the amazing women I met over the course of the two days I was there. Every single one of these mums inspired me beyond my wildest dreams; I felt alive and I was proud to be there.

To give you a good sense of the calibre of women in attendance, one of the ladies on my table on day one was Rochelle Courtenay, Share the Dignity's founder and Managing Director. The title she is most proud of though is 'Pad Lady'. She learned of homeless women going without basic sanitary items during their menstrual cycle and took matters into her own hands, collecting sanitary items within her local community and distributing to local shelters. As a result of this simple idea of giving dignity to women, Share the Dignity has grown into a national charity with some serious clout: Rochelle and her movement were key campaigners in the fight to remove GST from sanitary items here in Australia. See what I mean? I was winning already!

The day of my interview with the judging panel, I felt enormous calm. I was who I was, I'd done what I'd done. To help tell my story in the five minutes allotted, I'd created a PowerPoint slide montage of LBPR's journey all the way from lying in a hospital bed with Nate hooked up to tubes and machines, through to me in the LBPR office with my amazing team. The three judges were so impressive, yet still interested and supportive. I was very starstruck to see that one of these judges was Laura Furiosi, the 2017 AusMumpreneur of the Year.

When the awards night happened the following evening, I had no expectations of anything. Just like my first foray into awards with Illawarra Women in Business and the Illawarra Business Chamber, I was the underdog. There were fourteen national finalists in my category, many of whom I'd met. They were all amazing, achieving so much and making the world a better place. Just to be there was an honour.

It came time for my category to be announced. I'd joked earlier in the night with my beautiful cousin Amy who was my date, 'If I'm lucky enough to be recognised, I hope I come third.' Third place was a pink trophy and it was the cutest thing I'd *ever* seen. My boys aren't interested in pink, so I knew there would be no fighting over who got to keep it in their room!

'And in third place nationally, we are so thrilled to announce Lisa Burling from LBPR.' As Laura read out my name, I went into some sort of momentary shock. I couldn't believe I was one of the top three Rising Star Mumpreneurs in Australia. This was a moment and a sign that I was on the right track.

---

## Another little *unexpected* dream had come true.

---

It's important to say that, even if I hadn't received my lovely pink trophy, I still felt like a winner in the recognition arena. Since the AusMumpreneur conference, I have connected with over one hundred mums in a similar position to me. We have shared deeply personal stories, made plans to meet up and discussed collaborating together where we can see the opportunity. At the 2019 conference, I had the opportunity to speak and run a Little Dreams workshop for over 100 women. Sure, the pink trophy is special; but what's even more special is this new network of like-minded people I've found simply because I was willing to feel the fear and do it anyway.

> Little dreams centred on recognition lead to
> relationships, opportunity and connection.
> Never dismiss these as the domain of the
> egotistical attention seeker; the rewards go
> *way* beyond certificates and trophies.

### ALL IT TAKES IS A LITTLE GUMPTION: LITTLE STEPS TO TAKE NOW

I do hope after reading about my personal experiences in Part 3 you can see the enormous benefits that being open to opportunities and putting yourself out there can bring you and that you're inspired to give it a go!

My journey shows you that it's exactly that: a journey. I didn't even know about Inspiring Rare Birds or the AusMumpreneur Network when I started out. But I found them at exactly the right moment of my journey.

What are *your* little dreams when it comes to creating opportunity? Are they local or national? Inside your workplace or related to your industry? What about personal versus professional?

To help you, here's what mine was at the start of my journey:

> *My little dream is for LBPR to be recognised as a business going places, with an award from my local business community. To achieve this, I'll enter the Best New Business category in Illawarra Women in Business Awards by March 2015 and the Most Outstanding New Business category in the Illawarra Business Awards by July 2015. I will leverage this to make new connections and uncover opportunities for the business.*

Write down your little dream when it comes to opportunity and recognition here. Be as descriptive as you can and use the SMART framework - Specific, Measurable, Achievable, Realistic and Timebound - to make it tangible.

Refer back to the DNA of a little dream at the start of this book if you need some clarity.

**MY LITTLE DREAM IS ...**

_____

_____

_____

_____

_____

_____

**THIS LITTLE DREAM IS IMPORTANT TO ME BECAUSE ...**

_____

_____

_____

_____

_____

**I NEED THESE PEOPLE OR RESOURCES TO HELP ME REALISE**

**THIS LITTLE DREAM ...**

_____

_____

_____

_____

_____

_____

Now you have the little dream captured, write down at least four steps you can take right now to make it come true. To help you, here's my task list linked to my first opportunity little dreams:

- Speak to the business owners who won these categories last year; ask for a meeting and for their insights into what they did to be deemed the worthy winner (offer a one-hour power PR session if they need some convincing!)
- Draft the entry and ask someone from outside the business to review it for me to ensure I haven't missed any key points
- Contact four clients and ask them to provide a written reference on company letterhead
- Ask my accountant to pull together a P&L summary appropriate for this purpose
- Set aside time in my diary to write the entry (allow four hours minimum)
- Following the results, good or bad, connect with others in the category to discuss joint opportunities!

**MY LITTLE DREAM TASK LIST IS ...**

_____

_____

_____

_____

_____

_____

_____

All you need to make a little dream come true is a clear idea of what it is and some clear actions. Seems simple, doesn't it? That's because it is!

You can repeat this exercise for as many little dreams in the recognition space as you like. There is no limit - however, I'd recommend keeping it to a maximum of six. Otherwise you run the risk of veering into big dream territory and that's where overwhelm and inertia are waiting to greet you.

## Dream small and keep moving. That's all you need to do to make it happen.

# THOUGHT SPARK: THE CONFIDENCE CONUNDRUM

Let me tell you a secret. The more I achieved in life, the more recognition and opportunity, the lower my confidence levels got and the louder the self-doubt became. It seemed the more I ticked off the list, the more mountains I climbed and the higher I got, the less I believed I had what it took to do more. Do you know what I mean?

Interestingly, when I set up LBPR, I didn't lack confidence. Sure, I had low self-esteem and I felt shame, but there was a fire in my belly that knew I could do it. I knew I could make the business a success (and let's be honest, I had to). I knew that the way to do that was to leverage what I already knew, maximise the connections I had and *work damn hard*.

So why now, after achieving what I set out in a much shorter timeframe than anticipated, did I feel like this? I figured that I wasn't the only human who'd ever felt this way so I decided to do what any person with internet access would. I cracked open my trusty laptop, opened up Google and typed in the words 'the more you accomplish, the more your confidence goes down'. (If you want to see what I found, type these words in too but allow at least an hour to sift through, because what you will find is worthy of some dedicated time.)

I took great comfort in the fact that one of the links Google delivered was to the *Harvard Business Review*. This immediately legitimised my feelings; if one of the world's leading business schools had dedicated time and resources to this notion, there had to be something in it.

It turns out that Harvard has found a lack of self-confidence is actually the key to greater success and the reverse is a myth: 'There is no bigger cliché in business psychology than the idea that high self-confidence is key to career success. It is time to debunk this myth. In fact, *low* self-confidence is more likely to make you successful.' (Tomas Chamorro-Premuzic, *Harvard Business Review* online, 6 July 2012)

The author of this *Harvard Business Review* paper, Tomas Chamorro-Premuzic, has dedicated many years to researching and consulting talent, and he qualifies his finding by stating that there does come a point where too little self-confidence is pretty much as useless to success as too much. This is when fear and stress overwhelm you to the point where you're paralysed and nothing gets done. But just the right level of low self-confidence means you're self-critical and open to feedback; it means that your pessimism and ambition can produce outstanding performance; and it means others will more than likely view you as humble and unassuming, traits that are conducive to creating positive organisation and more broadly, cohesive societies.

Excitingly, reading this research paper actually *boosted* my self-confidence. I immediately saw that what I'd viewed as a major stumbling block to achievement was in fact my greatest leg-up and a resource I could use for good.

If you want to explore this concept further you can read the paper here: *Harvard Business Review* online: **https://hbr.org/2012/07/less-confident-people-are-more-su.** I'd love to know what you think!

# PART 4

## DREAMING OF ...

### BEING MY BEST SELF

# YOU HAVE ALL YOU NEED TO FULFIL YOUR LIFE'S PURPOSE

# 11

# Breaking

# Point

This is the best piece of advice I can ever give you. It's so obvious but, as we all know, sometimes the obvious gets lost and we need to have it pointed out to us.

**If you want to achieve your little dreams,
you need to be in top form –
physically, emotionally and mentally.**

Just like a racing car, you won't get to where you want to with substandard fuel and dodgy parts that aren't checked regularly. And there's only so much the team in pit lane can do if you're not in decent shape to start with. Similarly, if the driver isn't clear about the race plan or direction then it's game over.

For the purposes of this section, I define 'health' as physical health, and 'wellbeing' as mental health. Nothing – and I mean nothing – is *ever* worth sacrificing these two components of your existence. This is a lesson I've learnt the hard way, not once but twice, over the last four years.

The quote 'Entrepreneurship is living a few years of your life like most people won't, so you can spend the rest of your life like most people can't' is utter rubbish in my view. It sits alongside the word hustle, defined by one website as acting aggressively, especially in business dealings. No thank you.

After two personal experiences that saw my health and wellbeing reach their absolute limits, I no longer believe that you should have to push yourself to the point of collapse to be successful.

Perhaps a better quote to live by is this, my little dream: 'Entrepreneurship is doing something you love, to leave the world a better place than you found it, while nourishing your soul, your body and your loved ones.'

---

My little dream for entrepreneurship:
doing something you love, to leave the world
a better place than you found it,
while nourishing your soul, your body
and your loved ones.

---

Early on in my business journey, I was handed a massive health reality check. I want to tell you about it so you can avoid the near-miss outcome I had, see the moment of breaking point before you reach it and make adjustments to get yourself 'back on track' before there is no track to get back on.

I'd been pushing myself beyond reason in the first year of LBPR's existence to be better, to achieve more, to show everyone how I can do it all and still function as a human being. It's a facade that I managed to pull off for an entire year. I'd even tricked myself on occasion into thinking it was a sustainable existence.

It's partly because I have always been this way, and by 'this way', I mean goal driven and wanting to achieve. But, if I am honest, it's also partly because I'm a single mum. I hate the thought of people pitying me and, as a result, I put a lot of pressure on myself to show this reality doesn't affect me at all. Not. At. All.

At times, it's like I'm a competitor in the Single Mum Olympics. If someone says jump this high, I'll do it and then I'll create a new jump double the size, finish off with a one-handed cartwheel and perhaps even add in a javelin throw, just because I know nobody else will think I can actually do it and it will get me the prize.

During LBPR's growth phase, so about eighteen months in, I'd started to feel what adults call 'run down'. I'd wake up feeling like I'd spent the night wide awake, and most of the time I had, because I'd decided down time was not needed and I'd just keep that brain of mine on high speed 24/7. My iPhone was by the bed, my constant non-human companion, telling me what was happening and teasing me with its noises and light flashes to 'look, look, look' all night and into the early hours of the morning.

On the weekends where it was me with my boys, I seriously struggled to get to the end of it without feeling like I'd been hit by a truck. I didn't want to see friends as it required effort. You know, like having to pack bags and partake in a physical activity as simple as watching children at the local park.

This was not normal and I knew it deep down. But I ignored the signs my body was giving me to slow down and just kept on going. After all, I was super woman! 'I won't get sick and I can do it all!' That was my mantra and I was sticking to it.

Unsurprisingly, it got worse. My business was starting to win awards in my local business community and in the Australian PR industry. I was being recognised as a Businesswoman of the Year. Instead of stopping and enjoying this recognition for my hard work, the pressure I put on myself to keep going was on the increase. Once the stakes get higher, so does the pressure.

I raced interstate on three occasions in two weeks for work. On one occasion, I got to the airport, sat waiting to board the plane and, as I started to drip with sweat from the shivers, decided perhaps it wasn't wise to go and I'd best go home to bed. That was one moment in this crazy time of business start-upping where I did in fact listen to my body and made the right choice. My schedule would be punishing to my twenty-five year old self with no children, and any sensible person could see it was unsustainable.

'Slow down please,' urged my parents.

'I don't know how you do it!' said friends.

'It's easy! I just don't sleep!' I'd laugh and joke in response.

But it wasn't a joke. I hadn't slept properly for about twelve months. I'd eaten M&Ms for dinner every night for a week and thought that was perfectly OK because I didn't have time to cook and I'd make up for it during the day (which I didn't). I stopped making time for exercise and the things I enjoy.

Then it got even worse. I was working late into the night, as I often did, and I started to sweat. Hot and cold shivers. My left eye started to hurt and within an hour I looked like I had been punched in the face.

What did I do? Nothing! I ignored every sign my body was giving me that *I was not OK.*

'Remember your mantra! I am super woman! I do not get sick!' I continued to tell myself. I'd put make-up and my work clothes on in the morning and, honestly, I looked OK. Apart from a few comments about my weight and looking thinner than usual, nobody noticed that the flimsy walls of the sandcastle were crumbling from the inside out.

---

Little dreams will retreat if you let yourself get to the point where the flimsy walls of the sandcastle are crumbling from the inside out. Stop and recalibrate; like humans need oxygen to survive, little dreams need strength and sanity.

---

But then I actually got scared.

One morning, I simply couldn't breathe. My childhood asthma came back like a suffocating tidal wave and I felt like someone who had smoked three packs a day for forty years, literally overnight. My trusty ventolin didn't work – and it always works. I went to sleep for the next few nights worried that I'd stop breathing altogether. When you can't get air in your lungs, that's when you absolutely have to take note. I'd pushed my poor body to the point where it was literally on the verge of stopping altogether.

I finally went to the medical centre. The GP was not happy. He put me on a nebuliser (this is a machine where they pump pure oxygen into your lungs), told me my lung capacity was 38%, sent me for a chest X-ray and, based on these results, marched me up to the Emergency Department at hospital immediately.

The superwoman cape was swiftly replaced with a hospital gown. I sat there, a silly girl outside the Principal of Life's office who had forgotten to heed the most important lesson of all: your health is number one in *any* list of priorities. Without it, what's left? Suddenly, superwoman was no more. I had completely forgotten the most important task on the to-do list of any human being: you know, the one about remembering to take care of me.

I was a little scared. Actually, no. I was *a lot* scared. As I was tested and prodded and poked, I started to think thoughts that were devastating. I thought about the last time I was in the Emergency Department with Nate, and how I was there through no fault of my own and yet, here I was, in the same place, entirely through my own fault. I was no better or smarter than the man that stood outside the front of the hospital with his IV fluids, leaning on the pole, chain smoking before heading back in and taking up a bed that should be reserved for someone who genuinely values their life and wants to get better.

I thought about how much my boys needed me and that they didn't deserve to have a broken mum. I thought about all I still needed to do, and wanted to do, and that this was really not at all in the new plan I'd hatched just eighteen short months ago.

I watched people wheeled in and out, in beds and wheelchairs. I particularly noticed the people that looked like me, clearly dressed for work. I wondered what had happened to them in between breakfast and lunch that meant they were now horizontal and unable to walk. One lady who looked my age had a beautiful dress and earrings I own on. I looked at her closed, eye-shadow-covered eyelids and wondered if she was a sandcastle like me, crumbling from the inside out. I thanked my lucky stars that I could still walk.

The nurse interrupted my thoughts. 'You have pneumonia. All your other results are OK. You're allowed to go home, but you must take this medicine and you must rest. You are a lucky girl.'

There it was. A second chance. Handed to me like the most precious jewel you can imagine.

Whenever I speak to fellow entrepreneurs and/or business owners, it's sadly common for us to have a war story to share that's similar to the above. Some people still wear it like a badge of honour, like pushing yourself to breaking point is what 'the hustle' is all about. Quite frankly, I am embarrassed about it. That situation and the length of time it went on for is not the behaviour of an intelligent human being.

If telling this part of my story with vulnerability helps just one person stop and slow down – and maybe that person is you – then it's been worth it.

# 12

# BREAKING POINT,

# THE ENCORE

I naively thought I'd hit health rock bottom with the pneumonia episode. That was definitely a bad patch healthwise but it was not rock bottom. The *real* rock bottom with my health wasn't a slow realisation; it was sudden and completely suffocating You know when you're on a high-speed train and it suddenly enters a tunnel and it's so dark, so fast, that your eyes can't adjust and you literally can't see? When you feel your breathing quicken and your chest tighten? It was like that. And instead of my physical heath, this time it was my wellbeing and it struck me about eighteen months after my physical collapse.

At first I was utterly perplexed that I was actually feeling worse in my head than I did when my Nate was sick in the NICU, I was unemployed, my partner had left me and my world as I knew it had totally collapsed. This made no sense to me, no sense at all. Life was good at this point and I was truly back on track. I had no reason to feel anything but elated.

'What is wrong with me?' I'd ask nobody in particular. I didn't get this and I sure as hell thought it was totally unfair that I felt like this again. 'Screw you, universe,' I thought. 'You do not have my back, or my front for that matter. I listened to you, I worked hard and I got my life back on track. And *this* is how you repay me?'

Inside, I was the quintessential little girl lost. I'd been so busy doing – like Rabbit in *Winnie the Pooh* – I'd totally forgotten to feel. As it turns out, all the emotions I didn't deal with when I was in survival mode setting up LBPR were now back and demanding urgent attention.

On the outside of course, nobody knew. I was, and am, an expert performer. I continued to run LBPR and showed up for my clients and my team when I felt like I just couldn't. 'Get up, show up and never give up' was the screen saver on my phone for a long time. I loved and cared for my beautiful boys as always. I spoke at networking events and generally carried on like it was business as usual. At one professional event I spoke at, to my local business community, I was at my lowest ebb. I read from notes (which I never do), and it was all about sitting on a rock to work out the next mountain to climb, weaved in with questions about what success actually means.

It was, in retrospect, a massive cry for help. But with a lovely dress on, my hair and make-up done, and as the winner of three big awards at the same event the year before, this was quite frankly no place for me to crumble and speak my truth. I was honestly like a toy with fresh batteries inserted. Stand up straight, wind me up at the back like a doll, and off I go.

Every day was like walking through mud and that's one truly screwed up way to live, because what happens? You start to hate who you are. I convinced myself during this time that all I needed to do was raise two beautiful, respectful sons who valued women and who would be my legacy. That took all the pressure off, apparently. Now, Luca and Nate being amazing adult humans will absolutely be a huge part of my legacy, but it makes me feel so sad for this past version of me who felt that's all I had left to offer the world; that the only way anyone would know I'd been here on planet Earth was because of Luca and Nate.

I was totally convinced it was a physical illness I was dealing with. I wasn't accepting that perhaps I was a little bit depressed and anxious. So off to my doctor I went, all purposeful and Rabbit in *Winnie the Pooh*-like. Here you can picture my GP, a grey-haired Indian man in his seventies, looking at me from across his desk. I told him my life was busy, I didn't sleep well but I probably had some sort of untreatable illness and he needed to test me for everything.

'Dear girl,' he said in his calm, spiritual teacher-type way, 'you don't need medicine. You need a break. You're mentally and physically exhausted.'

Nope. Thanks for your opinion Doc but I wasn't having any of that. I demanded blood tests and mammograms and pap smears and, while I waited for the results, I of course researched on Google what was wrong. Helpfully, I narrowed the possible health issues down to an overactive thyroid, early menopause, an autoimmune disease, cancer or anaemia. Possibly a combination of all five. I was being totally sane and logical.

My results came back and, dare I admit it, I was almost a little bit excited to find out which physical ailment I had; something to explain that feeling. As it turns out, my doctor was right. My physical health was fine – lucky, lucky me – but I was mentally and emotionally exhausted.

These results hit me hard. I now had to address my wellbeing once and for all. It was time to dream a little dream just for *me*. In an area of my life I'd paid a price for forgetting about.

---

## LITTLE DREAM: To be my *best self* physically, emotionally and mentally every day.

---

My physical and mental health scares have forced me to realise that living life at top speed all the time is too much for my mind and body to cope with. I now know that, if you want your little dreams to come true, self-care is not optional; it's mandatory.

---

### If you want your little dreams to come true, self-care is not optional; it's mandatory.

---

I recently read a book by Aussie entrepreneur, Peta Kelly, called *Earth is Hiring*. She writes about play and how important it is; that we are born to have fun. I realised she's right and it was time to lighten up. I actually wrote myself a 'have fun today' permission slip that I laminated and left by my bed. I know – but I love laminating and whatever works, right? By starting to play more, I had room in my head to hear this from the depths of my soul: 'It's time to be your *best self*.'

If I was going to get to know and be my best self, I needed to first figure out what that looked like for me. Here's the list I made, which might provide some inspiration for your own list:

**HEALTH**

- Physical: healthy, strong, happy with where I'm at and my body's limits
- Mental: aware of my pre-existing beliefs and ideas and armed with strategies to deal with them
- Emotional: feel what I need to feel, but let it pass through me quickly.

**BUSINESS**

- Doing my best work, always
- Being fully present for my team and my clients
- Knowing when to say no and when to say yes.

**FINANCE**

- Working towards being debt free (except for my mortgage, remember the DNA of a little dream – I need to keep it realistic!).

When I looked at this list for my best self, I realised it was short and simple. I also realised I couldn't do the work on my own. Accountability partners are a big thing now, and for a reason. I am the kind of person who definitely needs this cheer squad to keep me on track; in fact, Luca and Nate were unknowingly my accountability partners for LBPR!

I called this 'The Board of Lisa Inc.'. I didn't include my family or my close friends because, although they are critical to my wellbeing and major contributors to my life, they aren't the ones who can give me that outside-in viewpoint that's totally untainted. And that's the view I believe the Lisa Inc. board members had to provide for this concept to work. I also recognised that I couldn't afford to pay everyone, so I looked into ways to ensure I got what I needed without needing to max out the credit card.

These are the Lisa Inc. board positions I came up with:

- A psychologist (for my mental health). This was subsidised by a Mental Health Plan which can be approved by a GP in Australia.
- A life coach (for my ambition). I found someone who was offering a three-month introductory course which meant I wasn't up for a massive ongoing investment.
- A gym membership and personal trainer (for my physical health). The gym I went with had no

joining fee and two free PT sessions as part of an introductory offer.

- A business mentor (for my professional health). The person I worked with only asked for a coffee in return for imparting their business knowledge and sharing their experiences with me.

It's actually really fun to imagine a big boardroom table, with you at the head of it, and picture the faces of people you want to be part of ensuring your stock prices stay high and that (insert your name) Inc. is operating at peak performance levels while remaining happy and sane.

Within a few months, I felt more myself than ever before. I noticed how spending quality time looking after me led to better outcomes in my role as a business owner and as a mum. I made time for the gym. I ate proper food. I made sure my eyes were closed by 10 pm at the very latest. I turned off social media well before I turned off my bedroom light. I got back into essential oils. Simple steps with a profound impact.

## A little dream had come true.

---

Why not create your very own board, right here and now? It's important to point out that your boardroom doesn't have to be filled with paid positions. You might decide for you it's your best friend, the dog and the gym instructor that leads the spin class you go to anyway. Whatever works for you!

### THE BOARD OF _____INC.

Today, I commit to be my best self - physically, mentally and emotionally. I know that I can't do it alone, and that it's OK to seek help and guidance from others who can help me achieve this state of existence.

My three areas of focus are:

1. _____

2. _____

3. _____

(Some examples include, but are not limited to, mental or physical health, spirituality, emotional wellbeing, fun, and relationships, career/business)

To achieve these little dreams and be my best self, the _____Inc. board members are:

1._____because they can help me_____

_____

2._____because they can help me_____

3._____because they can help me_____

4._____because they can help me_____

My deadline for appointing board members and getting my best-self project underway is date_____month_____year.

66What is more important than
others' perception of you is
your perception of your experience,
how you communicate and
how you feel about the energy
you give and receive from
the universe.
Always remember this:
people who try to pull you down
when you are being asked
to rise up are
irrelevant in your life.99

# 13

# Getting personal

# about values

Something my life coach and I did as part of ensuring I'm on track had such a profound impact on me that I want to share it with you in detail.

Understanding your personal values and their role in helping you maintain your health and wellbeing is something you may want to explore. I've found it to be life-changing and one of the most meaningful and powerful experiences of my life. These values are the 'wind beneath the wings' of my little dreams.

---

Personal values are the wind beneath the wings of little dreams. But if you're not clear on what they are, how do you know which way the wind is actually blowing? Take the time to find your values, so your little dreams can find *you*.

---

My life coach recently led me through a process that tested me to my core. It was designed to help me identify my personal values. We started with probably one hundred words and I had to circle all those that I felt were important to me. Then we grouped them together to create smaller themes. And then came the crunch.

'If you had to pick just one of these Lisa, and you can only pick one, which would it be?'

She knew how hard it was for me to answer that seemingly straightforward question. It forced me to work out which values were critical to the realisation of the others. I realised that not all values are created equal; some you can only fulfil by ensuring others are.

In the end, after a few minutes of 'I can't do this' and 'It's too hard,' it became surprisingly easy. The value that I can't do without, that has been subtly guiding my life and igniting my joy? Simplicity.

Now, at first, I laughed. I literally laughed a big loud laugh at myself because simple is not a word I would use to describe my head, my heart or the way I live my life. Chaotic is more apt and I do tend to gravitate towards situations and people that can make life incredibly challenging. But I sat with it and saw that yes, simplicity and me doing things that aligned with this value was absolutely fundamental to my mental, emotional and physical health.

I could see that reading books brought joy, that volunteering at the canteen for the soccer club brought joy, that building Lego houses with my boys brought joy (most of the time, except when I step on one), that sitting by the beach with a coffee in one hand and a fruit salad in the other brought joy. My little adventures that I take on my own whenever I can see a few days strung together were the holiday version of simplicity: being on my own, nobody to check on or consider, free to do as I pleased. I saw that catch-ups with friends in small groups and working on projects with clients who had a single-minded purpose were like fuel for my soul.

Yes. This all made sense.

So then, of course, I started to think about other ways I could bring more simplicity into my world. Because it's one thing to have your core value identified, but you absolutely have to live it and thread its essence through every decision, every experience of your daily life. As a well-known saying goes, 'Your words become your actions, your actions become your habits, your habits become your values, and your values become your destiny.'

I resisted my sudden urge to go completely overboard as that would defeat the purpose ('thank you, unrelenting standards, I acknowledge you and send you on your way with love'), but I did reignite my love for essential oils (I used them religiously when the boys were little but this daily task got lost in the chaos) and I decided to actually cook. People who know me know this is huge.

I decided to start by ordering from a meal-kit delivery company on a weekly basis and discovered that when I'm cooking and creating in the kitchen, my brain goes into a different gear, my phone is nowhere to be seen and my heart feels really full. I totally love taking photos of my version of the meal next to the recipe card. Yes, it looks like the 'nailed it' memes most of the time, but hey, I don't even care.

The complete irony of this entire process is my life didn't become less busy. I didn't stop doing things. In fact, I seem to doing more. Right now I'm leading LBPR through a very busy period, raising Luca and Nate, staying physically and mentally fit, and writing this book. I still see my friends, get to the gym and have a facial once a month (old habits die hard). I'm totally up-to-date with the TV series *Suits*. Yet I don't feel stretched or defeated or exhausted, and that's because I am aligning everything to my core value of simplicity.

By making time for the small stuff, life's little daily activities, I am seeing the bigger picture. By being completely present with whatever I am doing - putting my head where my feet are - I'm not distracted and I'm efficient.

Total alignment of self. My best self.

## The Power of a Positive Mindset

I'm lucky that I'm a glass half-full kind of person. I can always see the positive side of a situation … eventually! Yes, it took a little while when my life was turned upside down, but I did see the opportunity relatively quickly. I don't live my life believing I'll have twenty years ahead of me. Now is the time to be happy, to be grateful, and to just get on with it.

The same goes for the smaller curve balls – not everything goes my way, or as I expected, and that can take the wind out of my sails for sure. I'm human! But again, I see the situation for what it is as fast as I can and, from there, work out how I can extract the good bits. I'm not sure if this is my natural setting or if I've learnt to do it over time because I don't like wallowing.

I've read a lot of self-help books in the last few years and the common theme is this: if you look at life through a positive lens, it gets better. A fail-safe strategy I use is asking myself this question when something isn't working out as I'd hoped, or someone behaves in a way that is hurtful or unexpected: 'What is this situation/person here to teach me?' Once I reflect on this question for a little while, I can always find the lesson. These moments in life, where things don't work out exactly as we'd hoped, are the ones in which we grow and find out more about who *we* are.

Some other simple ways I keep my spirits buoyed include keeping inspirational quotes on my phone, lots of nice stationery in which to journal my thoughts, watching/listening to inspiring people (I highly recommend Oprah's *Super Soul Sessions* and *Master Class*) and keeping a journal where I can get all that's in my head out before it hits the pillow.

I also have an awesome set of Oracle cards from Helen Jacobs of The Little Sage. Entrepreneur and best-selling author Lorraine

Murphy gave these to me and I love them. Every Sunday night, I throw the whole deck on the floor of my bedroom, shut my eyes and pick one card to guide my week. The cards are always right!

You might like to try one, or all, of these techniques to see what works best for you. A positive attitude can absolutely make little dreams come true. It sure did for me!

## ALL IT TAKES IS A LITTLE GUMPTION: LITTLE STEPS TO TAKE NOW

I hope after reading about my personal experiences in Part 4 you can see the breakthroughs and shifts that happen naturally when you are your best self, and that you're inspired to give it a go!

Maybe you've read this section of my book and nodded your head intermittently because you've been where I have. Perhaps you haven't experienced what I have, but you sure as hell want to avoid it!

So, let's put pen to paper. What are *your* little dreams when it comes to your best self? Be as descriptive as you can and use the SMART framework - Specific, Measurable, Achievable, Realistic and Timebound - to make it tangible.

To help you, here's what mine looked like:

*My dream a little dream is to be my best self, physically and mentally. I will go to the gym three times a week, I will go to sleep every night by 10 pm, I will nourish my body with health food, and I will see my psychologist every six weeks, starting in June 2018.*

REFER BACK TO THE DNA OF A LITTLE DREAM AT THE START OF THIS BOOK IF YOU NEED SOME CLARITY.

**MY LITTLE DREAM IS ...**

_____

_____

_____

_____

_____

**THIS LITTLE DREAM IS IMPORTANT TO ME BECAUSE ...**

_____

_____

_____

_____

**I NEED THESE PEOPLE OR RESOURCES TO HELP ME REALISE THIS LITTLE DREAM ...**

_____

_____

_____

_____

Now you have the little dream captured, write down at least four steps you can take right now to make it come true. To help you, here's my task list linked to my Best Self little dreams:

- Join a gym and go three times a week
- Make dinner at least three times a week once the boys are in bed
- Meet up with my business mentor once a month, presenting an opportunity or challenge they can help me with
- Download the Calm App and meditate for ten minutes three mornings a week.

**MY LITTLE DREAM TASK LIST IS ...**

_____

_____

_____

_____

_____

These simple actions linked to a little dream have transformed me as a person. I am accountable to me and that's really the most important person to face – after all, I can't escape me! Seems simple, doesn't it? That's because it is!

You can repeat this exercise for as many little health and wellbeing dreams as you like. There is no limit. However, I'd recommend keeping it to a maximum of six. Otherwise you run the risk of veering into big dream territory and that's where overwhelm and inertia are waiting to greet you.

# Dream little and keep moving. That's all you need to do to make it happen.

---

## THOUGHT SPARK: YOUR JOB IS *NOT* YOUR WORK

I've had a big realisation in the last year that has had such a profound impact on my wellbeing. I feel compelled to share it with you in case it has the same effect.

My friend Michelle knew I was taking a road trip south and she snapped into action, sending me a message with a YouTube link. 'Lisa, listen to this as you drive – it's Oprah *SuperSoul Sessions* and she's talking to Jack Canfield, the guy who wrote *Chicken Soup for the Soul.* You'll love it.'

Of course, once I was out on the open road cruising along, with the trees my only view and the cows my only company, I hit 'play' and listened to Oprah and Jack talk about fulfilling your soul's purpose. It was amazing and I loved everything Jack had to say. On a couple of occasions, I pulled over to write down some of the things he said in my Evernote app so I didn't forget.

As I was driving and I'd already pulled over, I decided to just let YouTube go and see what came up next. Oprah introduced a man called Wes Moore, war veteran, entrepreneur, Rhodes scholar and best-selling author. I'd never heard of Wes; I am guilty of gravitating only towards people I know of, like Dr Brene Brown and Dr Wayne Dyer. But I thought, 'Well, this is either something I'm meant to listen to, or it's not. So I'll listen with an open mind and see what this Wes has to say.'

Once I started listening, not only did I have to pull over, I had to stop at a petrol station cafe, get my headphones out and take notes. Wes was on fire and I was happily basking in his flames of wisdom:

- 'We are not products of our environments, but products of our expectations.'
- 'The expectations that others place on us help us form our expectations of ourselves.'

Seriously! Where had Wes been *hiding?* I became his virtual girlfriend immediately. Little did I know he'd leave the best bit until last.

Wes moved seamlessly into talking about the fundamental difference between a 'job' and 'the work'. Now, I am not here to reprint word for word what Wes said, and I highly recommend you look this talk up on Google and watch it for yourself (have Evernote or your journal ready, you'll need it!).

Here's the sentence that gave me the clarity I was seeking around LBPR and all the other ideas I had: 'The work is not simply an occupation, but why you are here.'

As I've been moving into my new frontier, where LBPR is motoring along nicely and I am looking to explore other projects (like this book!), I've found myself in varying states of confusion. Wes's words made me see in an instant that my LBPR is my *job*; it's specific to my profession. Wes describes work, defined as the general efforts and activities done to accomplish a goal, as 'not simply an occupation, but why you are here.' It's linked to your legacy.

That *a-ha* moment, as Oprah would call it, was like someone lifting heavy weights off my body. Put simply, I thought LBPR had to *be* the life purpose, rather than a cog in the wheel that makes the life purpose turn. I thought that my PR consultancy needed to fulfil all my needs: the functional stuff (like financial security) and the spirit tingle stuff (that I'm working on something much bigger than myself).

To help me work it out in more depth (and I am a highly visual person), I created a sheet that allowed me to clearly show how my job and my work fit together. I look at it regularly, especially when I am feeling demotivated about what I'm doing on a daily basis, as this visual summary reminds me *why* I am doing it. I use it with people I have the privilege of mentoring to give them the gift of clarity too.

I know by going through this process of self-analysis that there is a reason I am really good at communicating and relationship building, which has manifested into a career in PR. Those skills mean I can share the message of my work easily; that my work can benefit from the talents my job has allowed me to practise and hone over two decades. Those skills mean I can earn enough money to explore my work with freedom and the absence of pressure that comes from deadlines and financial expectations.

Once this realisation happened, I found a new spring in my step in every aspect of my life. I knew that LBPR's success was critical to my work. Even the most boring tasks, like bookkeeping and renewing insurance policies, are now met with enthusiasm.

Wayne Dyer famously said, 'When you change the way you look at things, the things you look at change.' That's exactly what happened to me when I listened to Wes.

This example is exactly what I love about life, how a seemingly random talk on YouTube turns out to be the clarity I have been seeking. I believe there are no coincidences in life; everything contributes to your little dreams in some way.

**Your job:** what you do every day that you're naturally good at, primarily to earn money (for me: LBPR)

**Your work:** not simply an occupation, but why you are here (for me: to help people make their little dreams come true)

**Your legacy:** the footprint you leave after you die, something that lives on and makes the world a better place than when you found it (for me: my Dream a Little Dream project community flourishing and living on beyond my human existence, sharing the power of little dreams to change lives all over the world).

**The ultimate goal:** The skills you have developed as part of your job, enable you to fulfil your work, which in turn births your legacy. What a thought, huh? Let's dream little and make something BIG happen!

If you want to explore this concept further:

- Watch the Wes Moore *SuperSoul Sessions* talk. I dare you not to be moved and/or find something in there that helps you in some way!
- Create a mind-mapping sheet clearly showing how your job and your work fit together. This could be the most valuable action you do as a result of my book. I'd love to know if it gives you the same clarity it gave me!

# PART 5

# DREAMING OF ...

## A RE-IMAGINED REALITY

# THE GIFTS YOU'LL FIND IN TIMES OF CHANGE AND UN-CERTAINTY

# 14

One step forward, two steps back, or is it ten steps?!

Over the course of my just-over-four decades on Earth, I have come to understand that there are two types of experiences that intersect our linear human existence. There are the experiences that we proactively choose and therefore can control, and those experiences that we didn't choose and therefore can't control.

---

We can, however, take charge of our reaction to the experiences we can't control. And, being in possession of a heap of gumption, I – just like you – had to use it when 2020 came along!

---

As a self-confessed perfectionist with a clear-cut Type-A personality, I gravitate towards control. I detest being flung into a scenario where I Can't. Control. Any. Of. It. (I remember my parents and best friend throwing me a surprise party when I was fifteen. As much as I loved them, I absolutely hated the party. That was the moment I realised that surprises terrify me and, suffice to say, that was the first and last surprise birthday party I've ever been thrown.

The year after I put pen to paper/finger to keypad for the first edition of this book, I enjoyed focusing on the life experiences I *can* control. The best one of all was marrying my life partner, Colin. Yes, we found each other when I wasn't looking – of course! We got married COVID-style with only our celebrant Robyn, photographer Dave, my parents and our boys under a tree where we live – Colin's parents and family were on FaceTime from Canada.

I am someone who is never without a goal – either one that I'm actively working towards, or lurking in the recesses of my mind ready to appear. Marrying Colin marked the first time I felt fully supported by my life partner in all facets of my life, which in turn gave me the bandwidth to *breathe*.

Yes, just breathe.

You see, I'd been running so fast towards the next little dream, and the one after that, and that bigger dream far off in the distance for more than six years, and I'd forgotten to breathe. Physically and metaphorically.

What did this look like for me? It looked like a PR consultancy business that was stable and doing well, boasting a healthy bank account, which meant there was no need to push for bigger, better or faster.

It looked like me taking actual time off – proper email 'out of office' on time off – with my family. I read a lot of books and delved back into the world of fiction, after being addicted to devouring almost every self-help, self-care and autobiographical 'this is how I did it, you can too' narrative I could lay my hands on in the years prior.

Life felt good, and most importantly *I* felt good. Settled on board a ship whose course I had mapped out with my husband and children next to me, there wasn't anything that could up-end this blissful state I found myself in. Right?

## As it turned out, I couldn't have been more wrong!

It happened just as 2020 got underway. The first confirmed Australian case of the coronavirus disease – or COVID-19 as we now know it – was identified on 25 January 2020, in Victoria, when a man who had returned from Wuhan, Hubei Province, China tested positive for the virus.

Like most people, I thought COVID was concerning but transient and wouldn't have any real impact on my life. Modern medicine and the fact I lived in a First World country that was also an island meant the chances of this COVID situation impacting me were slim to none.

As we all bore witness to media stories from around the world showing the speed of the outbreak and the rising rates of infection and deaths linked to COVID-19, as government-enforced mandates like mask wearing came into effect, and as many of us found ourselves in lockdown for months on end with a dose of home schooling thrown in for fun, it became clear pretty damn fast that COVID wasn't going to disappear without a fight. When the World Health Organization (WHO) declared the COVID-19 outbreak a global pandemic on 11 March 2020, I knew the peaceful 'I am on this ship and the water is calm' life was about to disappear for a few months at best, or for years at worst.

My overactive imagination kicked into gear as a coping mechanism. It conjured up this crazy visual of all of humanity on a massive jumbo jet plane (hilarious really, considering all travel by air ceased quickly due to the nature of the virus and the way it spread), with a jolly flight attendant at the front of the cabin trying to reassure us it would all be OK:

*'Welcome to Global Pandemic Airlines. It's our pleasure to have you on board. Please fasten your seat belts. We are expecting some turbulence, although we don't know how rough it will be or how long it will last for. We don't know if you'll be okay in your seat or whether you might be flung about the cabin. But hey, we're all in this together so let's make the best of it, eh?'*

Back in reality, the virtual wheels of my new life were starting to rattle and the screws were coming lose. My PR consultancy business, LBPR, was the first element of my life to take a hit. As we worked with a number of multinational clients on events, the budgets were cut immediately. Zoom was still very much the domain of small children playing with Matchbox cars and to host anything virtually, other than a ten-minute team chat, wasn't a thing (yet).

I remember spending the first few weeks of 2020 watching the income of LBPR drop to levels I'd only seen when I started it … except now I had a team and an office and financial commitments. Work that was 'POd' (purchase ordered, the best reassurance you can get that an invoice will be paid as a consultant) was leaving faster than I could say, well, PO.

Put simply, the unimaginable was now here and I, like so many others in business, was caught totally unprepared.

I'd put on a brave face for my team who clearly knew what was happening but didn't have access to the full picture like I did. Nobody likes to be the bearer of bad news and I fully admit that I avoid having to share it like the plague … or the pandemic, as the case may be. Yet, in this instance, I decided to bring my team closer. There were only four of us and surely they had a right to know what was happening. By empowering them with the information I had, then perhaps they could also contribute to the solutions.

So, what did I do? The steps I took to ensure LBPR's and my financial security during a global pandemic are useful in *any* situation that is unexpected – those where we feel like we take one step forward, two steps back, or is it ten steps?! This was without a shadow of a doubt one of those 'things we can't control' human experiences, and, while a pandemic is a once-in-a-hundred-years occurrence, we will all inevitably have things happen in our lives that catch us unawares and surprise the bejesus out of us.

Of course, and I've already shared this advice, it's important to always remember that it's not what happens to us that matters, but the way we react to it. That's where we can step firmly back into 'things we can control' territory and chart a new course for our ship that might even be better than the one we had originally planned.

## DEFINING RESILIENCE IN UNCERTAIN TIMES

Resilience was a word we heard more in those early months of 2020 than we had in years. It was thrown about like everyone knew what it actually meant, but I think we can often miss the true meaning, to our own detriment.

So, what does resilience mean? Simply, it's knowing how to cope in spite of setbacks, barriers, or limited resources. Resilience is also a measure of how much you want something and how much you are willing and able to overcome obstacles to get it.

It has to do with your emotional strength and grit.

## PEOPLE FIRST

First things first – my team. I wanted to ensure we were all okay, mentally and physically. We immediately worked from home and I shared some initial guiding principles to keep us on track. We were all kind to each other. Kindness proved to be our superpower; it was the fuel that kept us all smiling and motivated when we were grieving for our office and time physically together. LBPR's values, which I shared earlier in this book, continued to be our North Star, but we adjusted their brightness. *Constantly Wow* dimmed a little, while *Stand Together. Always* became as vivid as Venus on a clear evening.

We also did a heap of online training; this was one of our major wins. Events that would have cost a fortune, required full days out of the office, or both, were suddenly available online and for a fraction of the price. The way organisations in the event space 'pivoted' (sorry, I promise that's the one and only time I'll use that word!) during this crazy time was commendable, and if their goal was to share and educate as many of us as possible, I dare say they smashed their KPIs out of the virtual park that year.

## REDEFINING LBPR

After exploring a total rebrand for LBPR prior to the global pandemic, which included a name change based on the fact the team is no longer just me and that PR is still misunderstood by many, I actually realised during this time that there was equity in LBPR and to discard it completely would be foolish.

Every cloud has a silver lining and this downturn in client work gave me the space to re-imagine LBPR, rather than throwing the baby out with the bathwater. I got to work refreshing the brand, which included an updated logo, fresh collateral, a new website and completely restarted social media (I will confess that Taylor Swift and her regular clear out of all her social media content was my inspiration for this decision), and commissioning research into current beliefs about PR, using our well-honed communication expertise to debunk myths and increase the understanding amongst our target audiences about the valuable – and arguably in today's world, critical – role that PR plays. In a weird way, the timing was ideal. It was time to shine and see the challenge of a global pandemic as an opportunity to invest in marketing for our own business.

My team also worked with me to launch a series of blogs, videos and templates that were designed to help businesses - especially micro businesses and SMEs (small and medium-sized enterprises) – maximise the power of PR during these unexpected and unprecedented times. We had spoken about doing this for more than twelve months and, wouldn't you know it, a global pandemic hot on our heels meant we had no excuses to *not* to make it happen. So, we got to work and packaged up decades of award-winning PR experience, making it all available for free online. I filmed a series of videos in my living room, changing my top for each one and telling Colin where to stand so I looked 'bright, not beaten'.

If you're interested in accessing this content, you can find it here: https://lbpr.com.au/blog/

## BRAVING THE BOTTOM LINE

When COVID drained LBPR's incoming work like a hole in a very leaky bucket, I decided to spend a full day in my home office working through the numbers and forcing myself to imagine the very worst-case scenario. I wanted to be an ostrich but my DNA is more seagull, so I committed to picking through the ruins and seeing what I could find to sustain the business for the months ahead.

---

If this global pandemic has taught me anything that will remain with me as long as I run a business, it's that you should always take the most horrendous scenario you can think up and double it, then operate on that basis.

---

I started by creating financial models that would ensure my award-winning PR consultancy could ride this almighty wave of cutbacks, uncertainty and panic. I forced myself to ask the hard questions: Where can I save costs? Where can I add value to current clients and ensure they continue loving us? Which businesses do I have some sort of connection with that could use some help? Where are the opportunities nobody else is considering?

Even though I don't like numbers (just ask my accountant), leaning into my fear and least-favourite task made me feel so much better. An informed business owner is a calm one.

## ALL IT TAKES IS A LITTLE GUMPTION: LITTLE STEPS TO TAKE NOW

When the proverbial shit hit the fan, I got myself into full gumption mode. So, what can you do when you find yourself in an unimagined reality that needs a healthy dose of re-imagining?

Here's what I'll be up to when (not if) the next unexpected occurrence hits.

## 1.  Execute like there's no tomorrow

As I've shared with you, we got shit done and done fast when we had to. Client work was either cancelled or postponed but, on the upside, postponed isn't cancelled and that just meant 2021 looked pretty good (fact: we just had our highest year of sales ever in 2021, surpassing the fee-income target we set). For our team, future planning was restricted to week-by-week and we had very clear deliverables. As the business owner, I permitted myself to consider what one month could look like. I firmly believe the five-year business plan is now completely redundant and twelve months ahead is all any of us can consider with some degree of certainty.

While I'm not suggesting you ditch strategic thinking, I am saying that perhaps sometimes the time you spend on a fifty-slide PowerPoint deck nobody wants to read anyway could be better redirected to actually creating and sharing the associated tactical and tangible elements of your overarching thinking.

## 2.  Get your own house in order

As I've also shared, I decided to focus on LBPR as a client. The truth is, I'd become like the hairdresser who never has time to do her own hair. If this wasn't the right time to sort out the LBPR marketing we'd spoken about and JFDI (just freaking do it!), then when would be?

We'd spoken about doing videos, how-to guides and blogs for the website ad nauseum. None of it ever got done because it just didn't seem important. But in this scenario, sharing these insights from the professional frontline also fulfilled our collective desire to give something back and to help other businesses, especially small and micro business owners, to implement our tried and tested strategies for retaining clients- and, where possible, attracting new ones.

3. Remember, we are all human

In the rush of day-to-day life, we can forget we are all just human beings. Like any business owner, my business's success relies on me being on point (the financials show where I've been healthy and happy, and where I've allowed myself to wilt) so I gave considered thought to how I could ensure I didn't fall down the exhaustion rabbit hole, one I've been down a few times (and which I've openly shared in this book). Clarity on what I need to fill my cup has meant my sanity has stayed (almost) intact and I'm ruthless about how I spend my time.

> Today, I managed to 'home school' my little boys while managing a bunch of client projects with my team. Who knew I had *that* in me?

Sure, it'll be a bumpy road for a while, but we will all get through it and we are getting through it. I have a feeling this will actually be a time we look back on with enormous gratitude. LBPR went on to win the Public Relations Institute of Australia's Small PR Consultancy of the Year for 2020 and I know the backdrop against which we were operating gave us an opportunity to shine. Wasn't it Billy Ocean who sang with gusto, 'When the going gets tough, the tough get going?'

He's right. After all, you can cut all the flowers but you can't keep the spring from coming.

# 15

## On the other side the new norm

As I write this, it is the end of the year and 2021 has shown itself to be a year just as challenging as the one before. In fact, I'd argue it's been a little *more* challenging, simply because we hoped for better and what we got was the same, and in some instances, worse.

A word I want to just plonk right here on the page is HOPE.

I think about hope all the time because it fascinates me. It's a future state, a promise of better times ahead, yet its effect on my mood and attitude is immediate. For me, and I know for many of us, hope is the fuel of life. Without hope for right now and for the future – for me, my family, my business, my close friends – then what have I got? Sure, we can exist, but existing is not living.

When the clock struck 12.01 am on 1 January 2021, I had so much hope in my heart. There was a vibe that COVID was 'so 2020' and that this year was going to be better. We'd all paid our dues with the pandemic police and this was the time we could really up the stakes on the little dreams we'd put on hold.

One of my little dreams was to take LBPR to the next level and so I decided that it was time to do just that. It was my virtual middle finger to the world and this wretched pandemic and hey, I love succeeding in challenging circumstances; heck, I set up and built a business in that scenario. *Why scale up when the seas are calm?* I thought. *Let's strap ourselves in and do it in the middle of the storm!*

I must be clear – the next level could be any manner of things when it comes to business. It could be more money, it could be more people, it could be more clients. For me, in business, it was all of those things. Buoyed by the public sentiment of screw you COVID, and spurred on by those around me, I did the complete opposite to what I had done just one year earlier when the world shut down. I ignored my own advice to imagine the worst-case scenario, double it, and operate on that basis. Instead, I grabbed a massive fistful of caution and not only threw it to the wind, I virtual sling-shotted it into the outer atmosphere.

I …

… hired *way* ahead of the curve – six people in three weeks – which meant more investment in IT equipment and office stationery (Kikki K will have noted a sales upsurge in those weeks for sure).

… moved into a massive office space that was very expensive, signing a twelve-month lease with no break.

… I started saying yes to every single person and/or business that approached LBPR for help (after spending years saying that I didn't say yes to every single person and/or business that approached LBPR for help).

… stopped sleeping because I was so stressed about being the perfect leader and business owner and making this all work. Because, if it didn't work, who even was I? Perfect Lisa was waiting in the wings to make her appearance, and I couldn't let Karen Patricia take the limelight she so desperately craved. (Karen Patricia is the name I give my inner critic – no offence meant to any Karen's or Patricia's reading this).

It was, in short, what my 2iC Lauren aptly named 'professional whiplash' and it was inflicted without careful consideration on not only myself, but my team, my darling husband who had to deal with my mini mental breakdowns at night and, most of all, LBPR's bank balance. I had created a monster and I hated every single element of its existence.

I was gutted, not least of all because I had made a promise to myself not once, but twice, and broken it. I promised myself I would never ever put myself in a precarious financial position again – first when I was a single mum who didn't want to ever worry about whether to get the grapes at $12.99 a kilo or not, and later when the global pandemic stripped out LBPR's confirmed client work like a whipper snipper trimming a hedge.

What ensued was months of chaos on every level. I spent more time worrying about HR than PR, I avoided the financial spreadsheet because the numbers at the bottom were all red, I woke up in a constant state of anxiety that my medication couldn't even suppress. I felt like a loser masquerading as a winner and that, my dear reader, is a very tiring existence.

> I came to realise that, in my quest for this so-called *next level-ness*, my supposed upgrade had in fact downgraded every part of my business and stripped myself of the joy I felt when it was small, nimble and manageable.

It got to the point where I didn't want to go into the sparkly office because I knew a total shit storm – either people-, profits- or procedures-related – would be waiting for me. It was, to be blunt, a very expensive mistake and one that I had to fix quickly, if LBPR was to survive. I also had to fix it quick if I was to survive.

So, within three months of going too big too fast, I went small, quick. Just like I had when COVID hit, I spent time looking at what could go easily. Apart from negotiating my way out of the office lease, the other area of flexibility I had was with staff. The truth was there were just too many of us for the work we had and the numbers didn't stack up. Slowly, with the support of my 2iC, we explained the situation and brought the team back to four people. I now know this is where LBPR does best in terms of size and I will never deviate from it again.

(That's a promise I make to you, my valued reader, right here, and you have full permission to pull me up on it if you see or hear otherwise!)

Suddenly, with those tough decisions made and acted upon, I had the space to define success for me personally, and for LBPR, now, in this new normal. Sure, I had many moments where I felt like I had failed. I'd ask myself how other businesses managed to make the leap from where I was, a staff of four with an income of just over seven figures, to multiple offices and eight-figure incomes. But that question is almost impossible to answer because we are veering into 'experiences we can't control' territory. And, as J. K. Rowling is famously quoted as saying, failure is important: 'It is impossible to live without failing at something unless you live so cautiously that you might as well not have lived at all, in which case you have failed by default.'

So, what does success for me look like now? Many years ago, I spoke at an event and explained that success for me wasn't an action or a thing, but a feeling. I'd forgotten that pearl of wisdom and only remembered I'd said that when I found the speaking notes tucked away in my journal. So, I started with the feeling of success and asked myself what this manifested into, if it was to become a tangible reality.

Here's what I wrote in my journal:

- I have a small team who I know well and trust to treat my business like their own.
- I am doing the work and almost 100% client facing! (I realised that I didn't launch LBPR because I wanted to be a businessperson; I did it because I loved PR, was good at it, and had the tools to make a go of it at a time in my life when I needed it to work.)
- I work from home, which gives me space to recharge and get work done (introvert right here!), and I meet with my team as needed to connect, discuss and plan.
- I have a good income with room to spoil myself and those around me without stressing *plus* a healthy gap between what is spent (expenses) and what comes in (income), which means there are never red numbers at the bottom of my financial spreadsheet (and that I once again like looking at it ☺).
- I have the time to be the mum I want to be for my boys, and the wife I want to be for Colin. This means being where my feet are and compartmentalising work and home.
- I read books. Reading is my happy place and I have set myself a challenge to read one book a week via the Good Reads app (look me up, I love having a virtual book club!). I know, I know, not everything needs to be a challenge – but this works for me.

I highly recommend taking the time to define your own version of success. Take a notepad and paper, grab your diary, type it up on an iPad – whatever works for you – and write down what your Success Signposts are. Or, you can jot them down in the template I've included here.

## *MY SUCCESS SIGNPOSTS*

1. _____

2. _____

3. _____

4. _____

5. _____

6. _____

7. _____

8. _____

Just like little dreams, you'll know what a Success Signpost is because you'll get that butterfly feeling like you did when you were a kid and Santa was on his way. The list will elicit a feeling of pure joy when you write it down and again when you read it back.

For me, the Success Signposts list I've shared with you feels like somewhere between a fancy pair of high heels and my trusty Ugg boots; it's comfortable but there's room for going out and kicking up my heels a little too without ending up with blisters.

You can have a life you love regardless of the external circumstances. All it takes is a little more gumption.

# EPILOGUE:

## Sir Richard Branson

I've read somewhere that you are the average of the five people you hang around with most. So, I often seek out opportunities to punch above my weight. Even if it's a bit scary to hang out with people who are smarter than you, more together than you, more beautiful or more confident. Terrifying in fact.

Sometimes, this concept can be taken to extremes. And I am without a doubt a woman of extremes. I am also a newly initiated believer of the view that, if you really let the universe know there's someone you truly need to connect with, even if it's punching so far above your weight it's almost laughable, it will find it almost impossible to ignore you; to turn its back on you.

---

Little dreams can involve people you'd love to meet.
If you let the universe know there's someone
you truly need to connect with
(even if it's punching so far above your weight
it's almost laughable), and it's because
it's related to bringing a little dream to fruition,
it will find it almost impossible to ignore you.

---

I'd been letting the universe know for just over a year that I wanted to meet Sir Richard Branson. I'm sure I don't need to state that he's a wildly successful entrepreneur and businessperson who heads up the Virgin group of companies and does a lot of good things to make the world a much better place than when he got here. Above all else, he is authentic, which means he is just who he is no matter who he is with, no matter the occasion. And, because of that, people want to be with him and be like him. People like me.

As I was building LBPR, I'd Google quotes from successful businesspeople and everything Sir Richard said resonated with me. As I started building LBPR, Sir Richard became, unbeknownst to him, one of my virtual business mentors. I'd check in with his publicly accessible views on an almost daily basis, to get a shot of confidence or confirm I was on the right track broadly speaking. I devoured his books and noted that he had started by dreaming small. The early days of his entrepreneurial journey were messy but he kept at it. He didn't let a setback mean a shut shop. My admiration for him seeped into my Facebook account as I'd post his gems. Friends started sharing Sir Richard quotes with me and one day a friend shared something that changed my life.

It was a post from an events company who were promoting a leaders' conference in Sydney. Guess who the keynote speaker was? None other than Sir Richard himself. I bought my ticket immediately and two beautiful friends, Bobbi and Cath, committed to coming with me. My aim was simply to breathe the same air as this man and hear firsthand all he had to say. I was beside myself at being in the same room, albeit a very big one.

The night before, I was lying in bed in the apartment and I felt this compulsion to mock up a photo of me with Sir Richard on Necker Island. I found a photo of him with a woman standing on the edge of a beach, pasted it into PowerPoint and put my own head on top of her body. Because it was so late, I didn't even bother making my head round and for those who know me, and the pride I take in my PowerPoint skills, this was unusual. I posted it on Facebook at 11 pm with the caption 'Tomorrow, I will be in the same room, breathing the same air, as Sir Richard Branson. If he ever met me and invited me to Necker Island, this is what we would look like.'

Lights out, phone on charge, eyes closed. Tomorrow was going to be a big day and sleep was needed.

&♂

We arrived early at the Sydney Entertainment Centre – a place that was usually reserved for rock and pop stars – and sat through a heap of speakers I really don't remember. I know there was a lot of fist pumping and repeating what the speakers said. It was really full-on and not really a style to which I was drawn. Sir Richard was due on last and I knew I wasn't the only one craving his understated energy. He was being interviewed by a local radio and television media personality, Ben Fordham. I knew that Sir Richard didn't like to speak and preferred Q&A-style appearances (of course I did, #stalker) and I was beyond excited to hear what Ben would ask this man, one of the greatest entrepreneurs who has ever lived.

Coincidentally, I did work experience with Ben at a Sydney radio station, 2GB, during the final year of my broadcast journalism degree. He worked there as the host of the drive program, alongside one of my good friends from university, Erin, who was the News Director.

During the day, I had many friends respond to my PowerPoint photo with Sir Richard. It seemed to have sparked something: a belief that, by putting this out there, I may in fact meet the man one day. Seeing is believing, after all. One of those people was my friend Erin. She was looking at Facebook for news stories and my news feed came up just as Ben Fordham walked past. 'What's *that*?' he asked her, which is fair enough, because the whole thing was a shocker.

'That's my friend from university, Lisa.' Bless Erin for firstly admitting she actually knew me; I would have pretended I didn't know me from a bar of soap, to be honest. She then told Ben about my life over the last few years and my love of Sir Richard.

Erin messaged me a few times during the day, asking how close I was to the stage. I thought nothing of it other than she was being a supportive, interested friend. As mentioned, this venue usually played host to rock and pop concerts; it was huge. But my friends and I were just to the left of the stage and kept moving closer to ensure I could breathe as much pure Sir Richard air as possible (bless my beautiful friends Bobbi and Cath, indulging my creepy obsession so whole-heartedly).

When he was about come on, I got out my blush and lipstick and brushed my hair. Seriously. I edged closer to the stage and, I kid you not, when he actually appeared, I took deeper breaths than usual so that I caught his exhale. It's completely stupid but, when you're older, and you admire someone, you do crazy stuff.

I listened intently as Sir Richard spoke of what his biggest learnings has been, what he's most proud of and his biggest challenges (at this time, his space business, Virgin Galactic, had just experienced a death through a test flight gone wrong and he was honest and open about that, which increased my professional respect for him even further). At around the thirty-minute mark, Ben seemed ready to wrap up.

'Sir Richard, you know we love you here in Australia and one of the common traits we share with you is our love of dreaming. We actually have a lady in the audience who has a dream to meet you. Lisa Burling, come on down!'

HOLY SH*T.

You know how your brain thinks weird things when you're in shock? All I could think as I edged closer to the stage was, 'I should have rounded my head when I did that crop on the photo of him on Necker.' Old habits die hard.

Finally, I get to the edge of the stage. The crowd is literally going wild as I move towards the man that I had virtually admired during one of the toughest times of my life. He stood up, walked towards me and gave me a heartfelt hug. When I say I met Sir Richard, what I really mean is, I hugged him, said I loved him and I even kissed him. I told him I was going to his home, Necker Island, one day (he actually smelt like a beach – and seawater).

It was quite over-the-top in retrospect. But it was all I could do to truly convey to the man, and the thousands watching us on stage, that this was a *moment*. Not some silly crush on an idol but a *moment*. I was just me, with him, in those fleeting moments of time we can't see passing. Me connecting with someone who, without a doubt, is very much above my weight.

The next day, my family and friends were thrilled for me. Even the local media covered it as a genuine news story. Ironically, my PR consultancy received a tonne of free PR as a result of this outcome.

Me being me, I immediately launched into a campaign to bring Sir Richard to my hometown of Wollongong the next time he was in Sydney, which was to be about six months later. My strategy was simply to do one thing every day that contributed to my goal of enticing Sir Richard an hour south of Sydney. I rallied the support of key influencers like the Lord Mayor, Gordon Bradbury OAM, who did a video with me inviting Sir Richard to Wollongong, which happens to be the official City of Innovation. I sent a personal letter to Sir Richard at Necker Island and connected with the head of Virgin Australia. Eventually, I was exchanging emails with his right-hand woman, who had access to his schedule during this visit. I could see that there was literally no time for him to come to Wollongong, without compromising another commitment. A little deflated, I agreed with her that we'd stay in touch and, next time he came, we would work something out. I am still on the case with that and, although I don't say too much about it publicly, I believe he will make it to my hometown one day soon.

The 'Sir Richard Branson encounter' (as it is now known) was a little dream that came true. Having met Sir Richard, something I thought was so completely unattainable, I started to believe there was nothing I couldn't make happen with my little dream approach.

# Acknowledgements

- To my beautiful little boys, Luca and Nate – I love you both so much; your presence and encouragement during this process has meant the world to me.
- To my amazing parents, Margie and Geoff – nobody will ever truly know what you've done, and continue to do, for my little men and me. Thank you for being my rocks, my confidantes and my cheer squad. I hit the parent jackpot with you both and I am truly blessed.
- To my husband Colin Blake – you arrived right on time and proved that good things definitely come to those who wait. I love you.
- To my entire immediate family, extended family, and close friends in Australia and overseas – there's simply too many of you to name individually! You've all been there on this crazy ride, whether

in person or virtually, watching me rebuild myself, cry and get back up, supporting my little dreams no matter what. I feel supported always and am so grateful for all of you, both near and far. Never underestimate how much your support means.

- To LBPR's team Yasmin, Stephanie, George and Eli, clients and my mentors. Thank you for believing that I could do it well before I did.
- To the New Holland Publishers team – Fiona, Arlene, Yolanda, Warren and Liz. You made a very *big* dream come true with this version of my book. Here's to book number two!

# About Lisa

Lisa Blake is a degree-qualified journalist and PR professional with over twenty years' experience working with some of the world's biggest companies and brands in Australia, the United Kingdom and Europe. She's the founder and Managing Director of award-winning PR consultancy, LBPR.

In 2013, Lisa's world was turned upside down as a result of a devastating chain of events. Refusing to accept her new reality, in just four short years Lisa has gone from an unemployed single mum to an award-winning entrepreneur, founder of award-winning PR consultancy LBPR and the creator of Australia's first student PR consultancy, Catalyst.

When Lisa's not making her own little dreams come true or helping others achieve *their* little dreams, you'll find her building Lego and playing trains with her husband, Colin, and sons, Luca and Nate, on the beautiful NSW South Coast of Australia.

Lisa Blake
LBPR1

randomactsoflisa
lbpr_consultancy
dreamalittledreamproject

Lisa (Burling) Blake
LBPR

First published in 2022 by New Holland Publishers
Sydney

Level 1, 178 Fox Valley Road, Wahroonga 2076, Australia

newhollandpublishers.com

A record of this book is held at the National Library of Australia.

ISBN 9781760794606

Group Managing Director: Fiona Schultz
Project Editor: Liz Hardy
Designer: Yolanda La Gorcé, Andrew Davies
Production Director: Arlene Gippert

Printed and Bound in Australia by SOS Printing

10 9 8 7 6 5 4 3 2 1
Keep up with New Holland Publishers:

 NewHollandPublishers

 @newhollandpublishers